No More Sharpening Pencils During Work Time and Other Time Wasters

Dear Readers,

Much like the diet phenomenon *Eat This, Not That*, this series aims to replace some existing practices with approaches that are more effective—healthier, if you will—for our students. We hope to draw attention to practices that have little support in research or professional wisdom and offer alternatives that have greater support. Each text is collaboratively written by authors representing research and practice. Section 1 offers a practitioner's perspective on a practice in need of replacing and helps us understand the challenges, temptations, and misunderstandings that have led us to this ineffective approach. Section 2 provides a researcher's perspective on the lack of research to support the ineffective practice(s) and reviews research supporting better approaches. In Section 3, the author representing a practitioner's perspective gives detailed descriptions of how to implement these better practices. By the end of each book, you will understand both what not to do, and what to do, to improve student learning.

It takes courage to question one's own practice—to shift away from what you may have seen throughout your years in education and toward something new that you may have seen few if any colleagues use. We applaud you for demonstrating that courage and wish you the very best in your journey from this to that.

Best wishes,

—*Ellin Oliver Keene and Nell K. Duke, series editors*

No More Sharpening Pencils During Work Time and Other Time Wasters

ELIZABETH H. BRINKERHOFF

ALYSIA D. ROEHRIG

HEINEMANN
Portsmouth, NH

Heinemann
361 Hanover Street
Portsmouth, NH 03801–3912
www.heinemann.com

Offices and agents throughout the world

The authors and publisher wish to thank those who have generously given permission to reprint borrowed material:

Figures 2–2 and 2–4: Adapted from Figure 31.1 in "Classroom Strategies to Enhance Academic Engaged Time" by Maribeth Gettinger and Martha J. Walter from *Handbook of Research on Student Engagement* by Sandra L. Christenson, Amy L. Reschly, and Cathy Wylie, editors. Copyright © 2012 by Springer Science + Business Media, LLC. Reprinted by permission of the publisher.

Acknowledgments for borrowed material continue on page viii.

Cataloging-in-Publication Data is on file at the Library of Congress.
ISBN-13: 978-0-325-05660-9

Series editors: Ellin Oliver Keene and Nell K. Duke
Editor: Margaret LaRaia
Production: Vicki Kasabian
Interior design: Suzanne Heiser
Cover design: Lisa A. Fowler
Cover photograph: Loskutnikov/Shutterstock.com
Typesetter: Val Levy, Drawing Board Studios
Manufacturing: Veronica Bennett

Printed in the United States of America on acid-free paper
18 17 16 15 14 VP 1 2 3 4 5

CONTENTS

Introduction Nell K. Duke   vii

SECTION 1   **NOT THIS**

1

No More Wasted Time

Elizabeth H. Brinkerhoff

Inefficient Classroom Management   3

- *Don't Mess with Recess*   5

- *Evaluate the Time You Spend on Classroom Management*   6

Lessons That Aren't Aligned to Target Learning Objectives   9

- *Does Daily Instruction Connect with Long-Term Objectives?*   10

- *Look Beyond Fun*   10

- *Respond to Learning Demonstrated the Day Before*   11

- *Evaluate How Your Lessons Align with Target Learning Objectives*   12

Lessons That Don't Engage Students in Higher-Level Thinking   13

- *Evaluate the Time Your Students Spend on Higher-Level Thinking*   14

The Essential Takeaway   16

SECTION 2   **WHY NOT? WHAT WORKS?**

17

Research on Maximizing Use of Time

Alysia D. Roehrig

How Do Students Spend Their Learning Time?   18

- *How Do Students Show They're Engaged?*   21

- *Engaging Learners Through Self-Regulation*   23

- *How Do We Support and Maintain Students' Self-Regulation?*   25

Classroom Management Strategies   27

- *How Does Reactive Classroom Management Lose Time?*   29

- *Clear Expectations and Practice of Procedures*   29

- *Classroom Community*   31

- *Not Just a One-Time Investment*   32

Instructional Strategies   33

   • *Poor Instructional Planning Leads to Lost Learning*   34

   • *Assessment*   35

   • *Instructional Routines and Procedures*   38

   • *Relevance and Choice*   39

   • *Specific Praise and Feedback*   40

   • *Matching Instruction to Students' Performance Level*   42

   • *Quality Tasks*   42

Student Engagement Is a Reflection of Teacher Actions   43

SECTION 3   **BUT THAT**

How to Maximize Academic Engaged Time

Elizabeth H. Brinkerhoff and Alysia D. Roehrig

Where Do We Begin?   48

Productive Noninstructional Time: Go Team!   49

   • *Whose Behavioral Expectations Are They?*   50

   • *Students Know What's Expected of Them and Do It on Their Own*   51

   • *Students Respect Others Because They Are Respected*   54

   • *Note About Procedures*   60

Productive Instructional Time: Let's Learn!   61

   • *Whose Learning Is It?*   61

   • *Students Feel Responsible for Their Learning and Apply Learning Strategies*   63

   • *Note About Feedback*   65

   • *Students Know the Clear, Specific Goals and Can Self-Monitor*   66

Working Together   68

Afterword by Ellin Oliver Keene   71

Appendix A: General Resources   73

Appendix B: Transition Ideas   77

References   79

INTRODUCTION

NELL K. DUKE

Not long ago I had the opportunity to watch a similar lesson in two different classrooms. In both classrooms, one portion of the lesson involved students moving from working at their desks to gathering on the rug as a whole class. In the first classroom, this transition took six minutes, in the other it took ninety seconds. The loss of time to this everyday occurrence, a transition, reminded me how much opportunity there is in classrooms to make better use of time.

Elizabeth Hammond Brinkerhoff and Alysia Roehrig show us how to identify time wasters and how to maximize our use of classroom time. Beth's experience in the classroom and as a researcher enables her to connect broad issues in American education to the specifics of classroom practice. As someone who has recently returned to the classroom, Beth wrote this book to communicate her intention of making good use of time in her classroom—and it shows in the very practical suggestions she shares. Informed by thousands of hours in classrooms observing both productive and questionable uses of classroom time, Alysia shares compelling models based on the practices of highly effective teachers of literacy. For example, highly effective literacy teachers have over 90 percent of their students on task over 90 percent of the time.

U.S. teachers are being asked to bring students to higher levels of achievement than ever before, and yet students are in school little more than they were many decades ago. We have no choice but to make better use of our time. I am so grateful to Beth and Alysia for helping us do so.

Acknowledgments for borrowed material continued from the copyright page:

Figures 2–5, 2–6, and 2–10: Adapted from Tables 2.1 and 2.4 in "Teaching Processes in Elementary and Secondary Education" by M. Pressley, A. D. Roehrig, L. M. Raphael, S. E. Dolezal, C. Bohn, L. Mohan, R. Wharton-McDonald, K. Bogner, and K. Hogan. (2003). From *Handbook of Psychology, Volume 7: Educational Psychology* by W. M. Reynolds and G. E. Miller, editors. Copyright © 2003 by John Wiley & Sons, Inc. Reprinted by permission of the publisher.

Figure 2–9: Adapted from Table 2–5 in "Focus on Formative Feedback" by Valerie J. Shute from *Review of Educational Research* (vol. 78, issue 1, pp. 153–189). Copyright © 2008 by Sage Publications. Reprinted by permission of the publisher.

NOT THIS

No More Wasted Time

ELIZABETH H. BRINKERHOFF

Early in my career as a third-grade teacher, I wanted everything done perfectly. And because everyone knows that "if you want something done right, do it yourself," *I* did everything. I washed the desks, sharpened the pencils, put students' homework in their folders, distributed materials, and organized the bookshelves. I did it all—and I was exhausted. Everything was as I wanted it, but my students couldn't have cared less. They didn't care about their materials; they didn't care about their desks; they didn't care, period. We were spending time together, but how productive was that time?

When we overly control our students' time (as I did) or, conversely, are careless about how we spend time in the classroom, we deprive our students of time in which they are actively engaged in work that matters, that helps them grow as individual learners and as members of society. If we want students to become adults who spend their time in purposeful, constructive ways, we need to give them opportunities to

What does purposeful, responsible learning time look like?

see Section 3

spend their time purposefully and take responsibility for how their time is spent.

"When I was a kid, the teacher told you to do something, and you did it!" Sound familiar? Years ago, our schools were run as factories, turning out people to fill factory jobs that were abundantly available (Horn and Evans 2013). In the twenty-first century, managing one's classroom like a factory means preparing students for a world that no longer exists. The "my way or the highway" style of management does not foster the higher-level thinking skills our students need to function successfully in a fast-changing world. We need to give them time to become self-regulated learners who are eager to learn, are able to identify personal academic needs and strengths, are able to monitor their own progress, and are deliberate when approaching academic tasks (Parsons 2008). Teaching is transactional: a conversation between teacher and student. Students' perceptions are an essential assessment of how we use our time with them. If they are not engaged, it is because they do not feel their time with us is well spent:

"Ms. Rodriguez won't care if I'm late. We won't even get started until half an hour after the bell rings. I don't like to sit and wait that long. We're not doing anything important anyway." (Tom, fourth grader)

"Ms. Allen is a nice lady, but the kids in the class don't respect her. There's a poster on the wall with class rules on them, but no one follows them." (Mariana, second grader)

"Ms. Hart treats us like babies! We can do most of this stuff ourselves!" (Jose, third grader)

"I need Ms. Barry to help me with this, but she has told the class that the end of the year is almost here and she doesn't have time to help us." (Roberta, first grader)

"We made robots in Mr. Gillis' class. It was just for fun." (Luke, fifth grader)

Perhaps these comments aren't representative of the students in your classroom; nevertheless, in today's climate of greater accountability for student achievement, all teachers feel the pressure to accomplish more in a shorter amount of time. With our instructional time dictated by policy, we surrender some of our autonomy and classroom time to things outside our control. Paradoxically, students spend less than half the time allocated for learning engaged in rigorous cognition (Fisher 2009). Expected to teach a greater number of topics in less time, teachers may teach for breadth rather than depth. Students reflect our watered-down instruction back to us with shallow understanding and disengagement.

Wasted classroom time is one of the clearest indicators that we have relinquished more responsibility than we should have. Three of the biggest time wasters are:

For research findings on how this time is wasted in classrooms across the country

see Section 2

- inefficient classroom management
- lessons that aren't aligned to target learning objectives
- lessons that don't engage students in higher-level thinking

We need to evaluate how we spend time in our classroom by asking whether it is proportional to how valuable the activity is in fostering students' independence and growth.

Inefficient Classroom Management

To some, a quiet classroom is an efficient classroom, but classroom management is not about keeping students in line. The goal is not obedience but rather constructive action. When students don't know what they are supposed to do or are asked to do things they don't think are reasonable (or can't do), they misbehave (or go through the motions): this kind of noise (or quiet) is a sign of inefficient classroom management. But the buzz of small groups working together productively is good noise! Kids know their voices are being heard. They're not disruptive but caught up in the positive momentum triggered by the thinking the teacher has invited them to do.

How can teachers establish classroom community?

see Section 3, page 50

Classroom management has to begin with community. Students need to understand that the classroom is *their* room: they are members of a community to which and for which they are responsible. Unfortunately, many see time spent creating a positive classroom environment as a luxury. Make no mistake: it's the essential foundation for all learning. Time spent creating a positive classroom environment isn't wasted. Students require guidance as they become social citizens in the classroom. Time spent talking, sharing, and learning to respect others leads to more productive instruction.

What teaching practices support students' self-management practices?

see Section 3, page 49, and Appendixes A and B

Students need help understanding what it means to be responsible for one another and for their own learning. We can make these aspects of classroom management—which have to do with self-management, not obedience—explicit by teaching desired procedures and routines. Anyone in a new situation or learning environment benefits from examples of constructive action. Students need us to label and demonstrate positive choices, and then we need to give them feedback on the choices they make. Teachers who fail to spend enough time teaching basic, noninstructional routines end up wasting time reacting to students' lack of understanding.

When this lack of understanding results in recurring noncompliance, both teacher and students become frustrated. For example, Tom drags his feet when his mother tries to rush him through breakfast. He whines, "But Mom, we won't even get started until half an hour after the bell rings. I don't like to sit and wait that long." His resistance is a clear indication of how little he thinks the time he spends in school is valued. It's not only how his teacher, Ms. Rodriguez, starts the day but also how she surrenders control to chaos throughout the remainder of it. She waits for students to settle down or to figure out what's next rather than giving them clear directions that help them get to work quickly. When students sense chaos, many take advantage of it. It's a way for them to show they disagree with the teacher's behavior. This is not the response Ms. Rodriguez wants, but she's unclear how to get the behavior she does want. Some interruptions are beyond our control, of course, but if we let students know how to handle them, we can minimize the time it takes to recover. A call summoning a student to the office to pick up the lunch she forgot, a reminder aired over the intercom about a student's ride home, an early morning fire drill, a special assembly—these interruptions are innocent and necessary, but they require regrouping, reorienting, and regaining momentum. We need to show students how to address the inevitable.

Don't Mess with Recess

Some teachers give children a longer recess as a reward for good behavior or take recess away as a punishment for misbehaving or going off task. Or schools may eliminate recess altogether to increase instructional time. In a policy statement issued by the American Academy of Pediatrics, the Council on School Health (CSH 2013) writes:

> Recess represents an essential, planned respite from rigorous cognitive tasks. It affords a time to rest, play, imagine, think, move, and socialize. After recess, for children, or after a corresponding break time for adolescents, students are more attentive and better able to perform cognitively. In addition, recess helps young children to develop social skills that are otherwise not acquired in the more structured classroom environment. (183)

The key ideas here are *essential* and *planned*. To be productive, recess needs to be regularly scheduled and give students "sufficient time to regain their focus before instruction continues" (CSH 2013, 184). (Effective disciplinary practices are explored in depth in Cassetta and Sawyer's *No More Taking Away Recess and Other Problematic Discipline Practices* [2013].)

Evaluate the Time You Spend on Classroom Management

I developed the tool in Figure 1–1 to evaluate the use of time in my own classroom. I was surprised to find that by reflecting honestly on how time is actually used in my classroom, I have already been able to recover about 30 minutes/day by tightening my procedures. In addition, I learned a lot about what my students expected or desired by considering my students' responses. The reflective awareness helped me to prioritize the order I plan to address my remaining concerns based on where I might recover the greatest amount of instructional time.

Try reflecting on how you spend time on the types of activities listed in Figure 1–1 or other more specific activities that you want to consider. Think about the possibility that things don't go as planned at times. Describe what actually happens and how much of the time feels well used. You may choose to record the number of minutes that you spend on each as Ms. Rodriguez has done in the example reflections provided in Figure 1–1. The times you record may be rough estimates, but itemizing them is a good way to start thinking about what actually happens in your classroom. You might also find a trusted colleague (or set up a video camera) to monitor how you use time during a school day. When you finish, prioritize the activities based on where you can recover the most time.

Reflect: How well do your students demonstrate ownership of classroom community, procedures, and routines throughout the year? What evidence do you have that time was well used? Were you surprised by the amounts of time used or how students respond? What's your takeaway?

Figure 1–1 Reflecting on Time Spent Establishing and Maintaining Classroom Management with Example Reflections from Ms. Rodriguez

Activity	Beginning of the School Year (first weeks of school)		As the Year Progresses (first quarter and beyond)		
	What actually happens?	How do students respond?	Priority	What actually happens?	How do students respond?
Developing and Maintaining Classroom Community (greeting students at the door; talking individually with students, etc.)					
Teaching and maintaining procedures and routines (instruction and practicing/reinforcing)	Students enter the classroom and wander around putting things away; this takes too long. (25 minutes)	Students talk and laugh. They don't sit down when the bell rings. They are very difficult to get on task, even after the morning announcements on the intercom are over.	1	I hope that I am never observed at the very beginning of the day because I can never begin instruction until about 30 minutes after the bell rings; the first part of the day is spent on pencil sharpening, attendance, lunch count, and other upkeep activities. (30 minutes) I haven't taken time to reinforce procedures and routines. I don't have time.	Students still take too much time to put their things away when they enter in the morning. I would think that by the middle of the school year, they would come in ready to learn. But students may be slow to be on task because they don't know what to do.

continues

Figure 1–1 *continued*

Activity	Beginning of the School Year (first weeks of school)		Priority	As the Year Progresses (first quarter and beyond)	
	What actually happens?	How do students respond?		What actually happens?	How do students respond?
Reacting to behavioral issues (correcting, disciplining, overlooking, redirecting, etc.)			3	Several of my students need regular reminders to be on task. (20 minutes)	Some students get up without permission, talk when they should be listening, and don't finish their work because they are off task.
Noninstructional activities during allotted instruction time (setting up, preparing materials, providing rewards or reinforcement activities, etc.)			2	Also, I have tried to use interactive student notebooks, but my students don't take care of them. I have tried to keep up with organizing their notebooks for them, but doing this is exhausting! (45 minutes)	Students' notebooks are sloppy. They don't take care of them. Maybe they don't understand the purpose for the notebook or have a habit for how to fill them out and when.
Transitions/noninstructional time (taking attendance, lining up, waiting in line, moving between locations/activities, visiting the restroom, getting a drink of water, etc.)					

When Ms. Rodriguez completed the reflection (Figure 1–1), she realized that sharpening pencils took about twelve minutes at the beginning of each day. Those lost minutes perpetuated themselves, like weeds in a garden:

- Standing in line to use the bathroom costs approximately twenty-two minutes.
- Taking attendance took another five.
- Lining up to go to special classes added an additional six.
- Lining up for lunch (including gathering lunch boxes and collecting money) was another six or more.
- Putting things away took about five minutes.
- Managing supplies was another ten minutes.

Ms. Rodriguez found over an hour (about 15 percent of the school day) of misspent time. No wonder Tom felt it didn't matter if he was late! But by setting up clear procedures and routines for these activities, Ms. Rodriguez can communicate to students that their time is valuable and show them how to spend it well. Clarifying and practicing procedures or routines is not time wasted but an investment that more than pays for itself.

Lessons That Aren't Aligned to Target Learning Objectives

Lessons that aren't deliberately planned to meet specific learning objectives are not a good use of time. Planning is essential, but some teachers have difficulty making the time and finding the energy for it. They may not realize the importance of planning. Planning classroom instruction is envisioning what's possible for your students and then being prepared to respond when your students don't meet (or exceed) your expectations. You can't

> **How can you plan to meet specific learning objectives?**
>
> see Section 3, page 61

predict the future, but you can plan for it. Some teachers do very little planning. They record what they did rather than plan what they will do. A well-developed plan combines long-term learning objectives with daily learning targets on the path to meeting those long-term objectives. When there is insufficient planning, it's easy to get distracted.

Does Daily Instruction Connect with Long-Term Objectives?

Ms. Barry continues her instruction where she leaves off the day before, but her long-term plans always derail. Instead of focusing on subsets of her long-term objectives with daily targets, she responds to whatever happens that day: if it rains, she teaches about precipitation; if someone expresses a controversial opinion, it's time for a debate; if the principal enters the room, he needs to be interviewed. Her fourth graders come to class prepared to be surprised; they know Ms. Barry often changes her plans. Each day is a roller coaster—they hold on for the ride, but they're holding on to something different every day. It's difficult for their learning to deepen when the concepts they encounter are so fragmented. In an effort to prevent this problem, many school districts have an administrator or academic coach regularly review teachers' lesson plans. But written plans don't necessarily tell the story.

Look Beyond Fun

Too often teachers don't take the time to think an idea through. A fun idea can lead to meaningful student learning, but only if teachers have structured it to do so. Students may enjoy gluing cotton on construction paper to make a cloud, but if the activity is not accompanied by higher-level thinking in which students synthesize the concepts related to cloud formation, it is a waste of time.

Luke has fun in Mr. Gillis' class: the students collect cereal boxes, cardboard tubes, yarn, cotton balls, ribbon, and other materials and create robots out of these materials. But Mr. Gillis doesn't explain what robots are and why they are important. When the principal asks Mr. Gillis what learning objectives the lesson achieves, his answer is, "It's just for fun." So when Luke's mother asks him what he is learning in school, Luke can't answer. And Mr. Gillis' students consistently underperform their grade-level peers on performance assessments. Although they'll move to the next grade level with fond memories of Mr. Gillis and their time in class, they won't take with them an expanded sense of their own abilities or greater understanding of the world. It's easy to be looked on as a party pooper when one dismisses activities like these, especially in a climate that is hostile to idiosyncratic, creative teaching. But idiosyncratic, creative teaching implies enhanced student learning—and that isn't happening in Mr. Gillis' classroom. If Mr. Gillis wants his students to create a robot, the activity needs to be grounded in specific learning objectives and designed to address those objectives. Perhaps they can learn some basic electromechanics and/or computer programming. (This may sound daunting, but type *fourth graders build robots* into your Internet browser and you'll find examples of elementary students doing just that.)

Respond to Learning Demonstrated the Day Before

Identifying specific learning objectives isn't enough. Instruction has to respond to students' needs, and students need to know how what they do each day adds to their growth as learners and people. We can focus so intently on planning that we fail to see, and address, individual students' needs.

As part of her planning for the school year, Ms. Ford reviews the state standards, the district's recommended timeline for instruction, and the available curriculum resources. She is overwhelmed by the immense task ahead of her. Instead of prioritizing what matters most for her students, she focuses on covering as much as she can within the time she has.

Knowing that her performance evaluation will be based in part on the achievement of her students, Ms. Ford carefully plans daily lessons that meet the objectives of each standard. She then dutifully delivers these lessons, which require little student response, day after day after day. Her students, bored with this monotonous instruction and frustrated by concepts they don't understand, begin to misbehave. Ms. Ford has to address these disruptions and falls behind schedule. Adding insult to injury, her assessments show that her students aren't learning what she's teaching.

For example, Charles can't keep up in math. Each day Ms. Ford rushes through an explanation of that day's concept. When she sees that a few students get it, she moves on, assuming that the struggling kids will catch up by doing that night's homework. Those who do catch up do so because they teach themselves or get additional help from someone other than Ms. Ford. Charles isn't able to avail himself of these options and falls behind. When Ms. Ford calls Charles' dad to complain about his misbehavior during math, Charles blows up: "That's not fair! She's a bad teacher. I don't understand anything in math."

Evaluate How Your Lessons Align with Target Learning Objectives

What actions can you take to align your lessons with target learning objectives and do you take them? See Figure 1–2.

Figure 1–2 Planning Checklist

	Yes, I Do	No, I Don't
I create a long-term plan:		
I study the state or national standards my students are accountable for.		
I identify the larger higher-level thinking skills the standards expect.		
I identify something authentic students can create or do that uses these higher-level thinking skills.		

Figure 1–2 *continued*

I plan what skills students need to practice and master to create or do.		
I contextualize these skills, breaking them into smaller skills that students can practice and master each day.		
I plan explicit instruction: labeling, demonstrating, and providing feedback.		
I explain how I will assess students' creating/doing (skill mastery).		
I adapt my long-term plan based on how students demonstrate understanding of that day's learning target:		
If students show they're struggling, I reflect and then reteach in a different way.		
If students show they've mastered the skill, I move on but monitor whether they're retaining and transferring their learning to other contexts; I add layers of instruction when needed.		

Reflect: How do you and the faculty in your school plan for instruction? Is it collaborative? Does your school leadership provide time for collaborative planning throughout the year and during the week? What human, material, and time resources do you have available to you (or do you need) to be able to plan as described in the checklist above?

Lessons That Don't Engage Students in Higher-Level Thinking

A major way our plans fail us is by not giving students the opportunity to engage in higher-level thinking. Despite small increases in total instructional time for all core academic subjects (mathematics, reading/language arts, science, social studies) over the past twenty-five years, teachers consistently report that they spend only two thirds of their time teaching (Morton and Dalton 2007). How do we spend the remaining third? If the time spent delivering instruction isn't used productively, what does that do to achievement outcomes? Literacy researchers observing first-grade classrooms found that only half of the students regularly engaged in learning (Wharton-McDonald, Pressley, and Hampston 1998).

Stand-and-deliver instruction, in which students listen and teachers lecture, does not foster deep learning. Students need to be able to explore while learning. They need a daily balanced diet of direct whole-class instruction, small-group instruction and practice, collaborative work, individual instruction, independent practice, and assessment. How much time students spend focused on what we expect them to learn is key.

Ms. June aligns her objectives and assessments with the curricular standards for kindergarten and begins to plan her learning activities. "This is kindergarten," she thinks. "Students need to know the letters of the alphabet and their corresponding sounds." She wants her students to learn the letter *B*. To do so, they will write *B* while making its corresponding sound. They will sort items (pictures) that begin with the sound of the letter *B* and those that don't. Finally, they will string bead necklaces at one learning center (the word *beads* begins with the letter *B*) and glue macaroni to a piece of paper in the shape of a *B* at another.

Will her students learn the letter *B* and the corresponding sound? Some will, certainly. But Phoebe—who loves Ms. June, thinks kindergarten is fun, and loves to string beads—thinks, "I can give this necklace to Mommy. She will like it so much!" She doesn't associate making the necklace with learning the letter *B*, and when the lesson is over she doesn't know the sound associated with it. The time she has spent stringing beads could have been better used.

Evaluate the Time Your Students Spend on Higher-Level Thinking

Who is doing what during instructional time? How does what you planned play out? Figure 1–3 provides some general instructional delivery formats that you might use and some reflective prompts to help you evaluate how well students' higher-level thinking was supported. You can create a similar table for yourself with more specifics, perhaps just by adding columns to your own lesson plans.

Figure 1–3 Instructional Delivery

	Minutes Planned	What Actually Happens? (Sometimes things don't go as planned or learning activities don't meet the instructional objective.)	How Do Students Respond? (Do they appear on task and excited about tasks? Are they off task or distracted?)	Minutes Spent Doing Higher-Level Thinking
Direct instruction (whole-group lecture/ teacher talks most)				
Small-group practice and instruction				
Collaborative work (students working with peers, teacher facilitates)				
Individual instruction				

continues

Figure 1–3 *continued*

	Minutes Planned	What Actually Happens?	How Do Students Respond?	Minutes Spent Doing Higher-Level Thinking
Independent practice				
Assessment (formative, to monitor learning and adjust teaching, or summative, to evaluate student proficiency after a unit)				

Reflect: Do students spend more time doing than you spend giving direct instruction?

The Essential Takeaway

We have reviewed our actual use of time in our classrooms. Already, we can see where time may be regained. We are reminded that our instruction needs to include opportunities for students to take responsibility for their learning. Teaching them how to monitor their progress, identify personal learning goals, and focus their attention on their areas of weakness takes time, but this time is recoverable: we'll spend less time motivating students and trying to keep them on task when they recognize the value of their learning. In Section 2, Alysia will help us to understand what research suggests is best for increasing our productive use of time in the classroom. Then in Section 3, Alysia and I will provide practical guidance on how to implement a number of time-enhancing strategies.

WHY NOT? WHAT WORKS?

Research on Maximizing Use of Time

ALYSIA D. ROEHRIG

We can think about the use of time in schools by teachers and students in many different ways, and many have (for a review see Berliner 1990). In fact, the variety of ways researchers have categorized instructional time can make it very difficult to compare and apply them. However, it is important to push beyond the jargon because how we think about and describe time likely influences how we use it! One common thread is the loss of instructional time to transitions, behavioral distractions, and poorly planned learning activities. Although some teachers claim they have little control over student success, attributing students' behavior and learning differences to their home lives (Tschannen-Moran, Hoy, and Hoy 1998), the amount of time children spend in school suggests otherwise. After sleeping, children spend the largest proportion of their time in school (Hofferth and Sandberg 2001). Based on time alone, teachers' scope of influence is bigger than we may think. In Section 1, Beth argued that we can make more time by not wasting it, which requires that we be more mindful of how we use time. In this section, I provide an overview of key understandings, activities, and strategies for maximizing learning time, beginning with time allocation, then classroom management and instruction, and ending with the ultimate goal—student engagement. The management and instructional strategies I highlight work to support one another and students' motivation to participate in learning activities.

How Do Students Spend Their Learning Time?

Within the given school calendar and day, there is time that states or districts might require teachers to schedule, for example, a ninety-minute reading block. (See Figure 2–1 and Kolbe, Partridge, and O'Reilly [2011] for more "time in school" statistics.) Then, there is the time that you, the teacher, plan for instruction on a curriculum topic (as opposed to the actual time you end up spending on it; e.g., see how much time teachers report teaching specific subjects on the Schools and Staffing Survey [Dee, Jacob, and Schwartz 2013]). But how much time in a school day is well spent? How much more time lies waiting misused or overlooked? Just because time was allotted to instruction doesn't mean it was all used as planned or planned well. In Section 1, the amount of time Ms. Rodriguez identified as wasted in a given day, the minutes not spent on activities that matter to students' growth, could add up to more than one hundred hours in a school year! That is

Figure 2–1 Time in School Statistics

- Most traditional public schools in the United States operate on a traditional calendar (fall to early summer) of approximately 180 days and on average 6.75 hours per day.

- Charter and private school days last on average 10–15 minutes longer.

- Time requirements differ by state and grade.

- Minimum instructional days required range from 160–186 per year.

- Minimum allowable hours per day range from 5.5 to 7 hours per day.

(Kolbe, Partridge, and O'Reilly 2011)

the equivalent of more than 3 weeks of instructional time during the average school year in a public elementary school following a traditional school calendar.

Want to see what it looks like when Ms. Rodriguez makes better use of her time?

see Section 3, page 67

It's essential to understand that the time you spend delivering instruction is not necessarily equal to the time students spend learning. While you deliver instruction, your students may be quiet and appear to be listening to you talk, but how well do students' actions reflect what we want them to be learning? As Beth explained in Section 1, teaching is transactional: the actions teachers take influence students' behaviors and understanding, which also influence the actions teachers take. The time that teachers have and spend delivering instruction and the time that students are actively demonstrating their understanding are different categories of time that we need to measure. See Figure 2–2 for the categories of learning time identified by researchers.

Figure 2–2 Five Categories of Learning Time

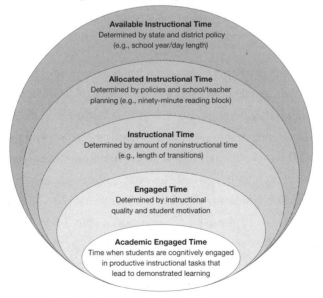

Adapted from Figure 31.1 in Gettinger and Walter (2012)

In Section 1, what was happening in the classroom did not reflect an awareness of students' needs and engagement. How do you monitor for these indicators?

see Section 3, page 64

As you reflect on the ways you use your time and what might be optimal, it is important to point out that the exact amount and kind of learning time needed varies greatly—between students, teachers, and grade levels. It depends on three factors: the student's needs and current performance level, the quality of the instruction, and how engaged the student is in the instruction (see Figure 2–3). For example, students who enter first grade with lower vocabulary skills need more code-focused instruction to make gains in word-reading skills than students who start with higher levels of vocabulary skill (Connor et al. 2007, 2009).

Figure 2–3 How Students Should Spend Their Learning Time

How students should spend their learning time depends on:

- students' needs and current performance level

- quality of the instruction

- how engaged students are in the instruction.

Research suggests that spending more time on small-group (as opposed to whole-class) instruction is associated with better gains in students' reading achievement. Carlisle and Berebitsky (2011) compared the outcomes of schools that had reading coaches and professional development to schools that had only professional development. They found that if teachers perceived they had greater principal support for change *regardless of whether they had a coach or not* they did more small-group, differentiated instruction; moreover, the odds that students would be labeled as at risk for low reading ability at the end of the year decreased! Research on effective schools supports similar conclusions. Taylor and her colleagues (2000) collected extensive classroom observations as well as logs of teachers' instructional activities and teacher surveys to compare schools with primary-grade teachers who were more or less effective in terms of their students' reading achievement. In the most effective schools (as compared to less effective schools), time and support were provided for small-group instruction; teachers spent more time overall on reading instruction; teachers also spent twice as much time on small-group (as opposed to whole-class) primary-grade reading instruction (this research and guidance for practitioners can be found in *Catching Schools* by Taylor [2011]).

Nevertheless, it is impossible to prescribe the optimal amounts of time to spend on specific instructional activities, with every child, in every content area throughout the day and school year. Thus, I caution against rigidly implementing specific amounts of time (such as those identified by Taylor [2011]) as a prescription—without being responsive to assessments of students' learning, you would be unable to adjust your plans to meet your students' needs. Small-group instruction is particularly powerful because it allows you to differentiate instruction for students in a responsive fashion. The amounts of time on different types of instruction should be individualized in consideration of students' zone of proximal development (ZPD), which represents what learners can do beyond their current skill level with the help of a more knowledgeable other like a teacher or peer (Vygotsky 1978).

How Do Students Show They're Engaged?

As a researcher, one of the most important lessons I have learned—from talking with and observing dozens of teachers over the years—is that promoting academic engaged time is not easy. There are many resources out there to assist you with selecting learning activities that are aligned with your objectives (and/or the Common Core State Standards) and support students' success on assessments measuring these objectives (see Section 3 and Appendix A for some resources). The problem is that guidance is often lacking about how to optimize the time you have to spend on these learning activities and increase the chances that your students are deeply engaged in the tasks.

Student engagement is more than appearing occupied with the task at hand, and it isn't about measuring how much fun students appear to be having. I think the breadth and depth of the concept of engagement is captured in the following quotation describing engaged reading:

> Devoted students are intent on reading to understand. They focus on meaning and avoiding distractions. Strategies such as self-monitoring and inferencing are used with little effort. These readers exchange ideas and interpretations with fellow students. We refer to such students, those who are intrinsically motivated to read for knowledge and enjoyment, as "engaged" readers. (Guthrie 2001, para. 1)

Intent, focus, exchange—these words reflect strategic student action and understanding of the authentic purpose of their task. Students need more "engaged time spent on targeted tasks that have clear instructional or learning goals" (Gettinger and Walter 2012, 663).

Engagement has more generally been described as students not just appearing to be procedurally engaged (as in they look like they are doing what you expect them to do) but actually being engaged in the kinds of cognitive processing needed for learning to occur. Cognitive processing involves the mental capacities and actions associated with learning—including our attention, encoding, and organization of information, as well as storage and retrieval of information from memory (Schunk 2008). Cognitive engagement, or academic learning time, is intertwined with concepts of cognitive processing as well as motivation. Berliner (1990) talked about the intersection of time and a student's motivation as *perseverance*: "the amount of time a student is willing to spend on learning a task or unit of instruction. This is measured as engagement, or the time-on-task that the student willingly puts into learning" (6).

Although cognitive processing is practically impossible for us to observe, we can create learning activities that provide an opportunity for students to share what they are thinking, such as when students learn about and apply self-questioning strategies about what they are reading (e.g., as part of reciprocal teaching [Palincsar and Brown 1984]; also see such strategies applied in science [Michalsky, Mevarech, and Haibi 2013]) or when they "compare new information against prior understanding" (McLaughlin et al. 2005, 4). So, although one size (time) does not fit all, students' achievement is better predicted by the amount of "academic engaged time" than by the amount of time allocated for instruction. Students' engagement can be monitored at many levels using different indicators, including, for example, whether students stay on task, participate enthusiastically, and can successfully complete higher-level learning activities or assignments (also see assessment tools in Appendix A).

Engaging Learners Through Self-Regulation

Motivation and self-regulation are two interconnected indicators of engagement, so I'll talk about them together. Motivation can be thought of as that which inspires us to action, no matter where the reason for that desire or drive comes from. Self-regulation, on the other hand, is a process that incorporates both motivation and metacognition (thinking about your thinking); self-regulation involves the ways we evaluate and manage our performances and goals, then change them as needed to meet desired outcomes. Hence, both motivation and self-regulation are important to support students if we want them to be successful in the learning process (for a further review and a look at how to motivate students' literacy learning, see Roehrig et al. [2013]).

That is not to say that students need to be extrinsically (i.e., externally) motivated by teachers who offer treats and stickers in a way that can be perceived as controlling (for more on control versus support, see Roehrig et al. [2013]); in fact, that is generally counterproductive for learning. To remain engaged in learning, students need to employ self-regulation strategies, and they need to be motivated to employ self-regulation strategies as well! Most of the time-saving strategies you'll learn here and in Section 3 are built on the understanding that students need support to maintain or develop their intrinsic (i.e., internal) motivation to learn. In addition, learners' perception of the control they have over their learning can also help them maintain or develop their intrinsic motivation—if students do not feel they have some sort of control over their behavior and learning, they will not have the opportunity to learn how to regulate their own behaviors and learning. Students who have a sense of autonomy are more likely to be intrinsically motivated and self-regulated (Pintrich and De Groot 1990; Pulfrey, Darnon, and Butera 2013; Vansteenkiste et al. 2004). They have the motivation to carry out self-regulated activities, such as checking their work, completing homework, and so on (see Ryan and Deci [2000] on self-determination theory).

Helping students to become self-regulated in their learning and behavior is the central mechanism for supporting effective instruction and classroom management. The trick is how to get students to set their learning goals, deploy appropriate strategies to achieve their goals, monitor their learning and behavior, and adjust their strategies along the way. It is necessary to explicitly teach, model, and practice strategies and procedures for each of the parts of the self-regulation process. These were likely the things missing in Ms. Hart's classroom management and in Ms. Ford's classroom instruction. Self-regulation is the anti–assembly line model for education. It can help students develop the skills needed to manage their learning of increasingly complex concepts and content as they proceed through school and into adulthood—it is the basis of lifelong learning (Lüftenegger et al. 2012). Moreover, choice is a key component of learning to self-regulate (how can students learn to make decisions about applying strategies if they never have opportunities to make choices?), as well as a key component in maintaining the high levels of motivation and engagement needed to sustain regulatory processes and learning.

The experiment conducted by Cordova and Lepper (1996) provides a dramatic example of the role of choice in elementary school students' mathematics learning. The authors randomly assigned fourth- and fifth-grade students to different instructional conditions provided by a computer game targeting the same order-of-operations learning objective. The instructional conditions were varied by the researchers to provide some students with abstract instruction (control group) and other students with different fantasy contexts (such as imagining they were traveling to other planets to solve Earth's energy crisis), choices (or no choices) about names and icons in the fantasy, and/or personalization (or no personalization) of the instruction with students' names and other relevant referents. What they found was dramatic! Contextualizing and personalizing instruction increased students' motivation, engagement, learning, sense of competence, and desired level of future challenge. But providing choices, on top of personalizing and contextualizing with the fantasy setting, led to even better outcomes! Cordova and Lepper (1996) explained the results this way: "[Students] became more deeply involved in the activities, attempting to use more complex operations, and thereby learned more from the activities in a fixed period of time" (726). Just think about how much more learning can be achieved with such intensity of engagement!

How Do We Support and Maintain Students' Self-Regulation?

There are three categories—classroom atmosphere, instruction, and management—teachers can focus on to support and maintain students' self-regulation as learners (Pressley, Dolezal, Raphael, Mohan, Roehrig, and Bogner 2003; Roehrig and Christesen 2010). Each of the three elements is necessary but alone is not sufficient to keep the majority of your students engaged most of the time. A teacher may have great instructional content and teaching strategies, but if classroom management is a problem, her students may not be apt to pay attention to instruction. Likewise, the classroom atmosphere can support the willingness of students to engage in learning and not create behavior management problems.

Figure 2–4 Strategies for Maximizing Academic Engaged Time

Classroom Management Strategies (Productive Use of Noninstructional Time)	Instructional Strategies (Productive Use of Instructional Time)	Student-Mediated Strategies (Engaging Learners via Self-Regulation)	
• Establish a classroom learning community.	• Allow students to have some choice in their learning. • Help students see the relevance in their learning.	• Have students set their own goals for learning.	**Causally/Temporally Related Strategies**
• Establish consistent and efficient classroom routines.	• Establish consistent and efficient classroom routines.	• Establish consistent and efficient classroom routines.	
• Monitor student behavior. • Provide practice and reinforcement for following routines.	• Use technology-assisted assessments efficiently. • Provide frequent, specific feedback.	• Incorporate self-monitoring procedures in the classroom.	
• Minimize classroom disruptions and off-task behavior.	• Use advance organizers. • Facilitate active student responding. • Focus on explicit learning objectives. • Match instruction with students' abilities. • Use multiple teaching methods. • Ensure that students understand directions.	• Teach students to employ metacognitive and study strategies. • Use homework effectively to enhance student learning.	
• Reduce transition time.	• Deliver instruction at a quick, smooth, and efficient pace.	• Support students' self-management skills.	

Mutually Reinforcing Strategies

Adapted from Table 31.1 in Gettinger and Walter (2012, 662)

In Figure 2–4, I outline research-based strategies for instructional and noninstructional time that are frequently interconnected and are organized in a possible sequence. For example, it is hard to establish an authentically caring and respectful learning community with your students if you don't allow students to have some choices, help make learning relevant to them, and assist them in setting their own goals. As you continue reading this section, you'll see how classroom management and instructional strategies include and reinforce student-mediated strategies.

Classroom Management Strategies

Classroom management is one of the most difficult parts of a teacher's job and is something even experienced teachers often continue to find very challenging and stressful (Clunies-Ross, Little, and Kienhuis 2008). We don't yet know how much time should be spent on what I call "productive noninstructional time," like time spent building a caring classroom community, or practicing routines, and so on, but we do know that it's necessary. The quality of teacher-student interactions, including a positive emotional climate in the classroom and use of proactive classroom management (e.g., Hamre et al. 2013; Pianta et al. 2008), leads to higher rates of time on task or task engagement (e.g., Evertson 1989) and learning for students (e.g., Freiberg, Stein, and Huang 1995; Hamre and Pianta 2005). For example, Hamre and Pianta followed young students who differed in their levels of risk for school failure based on demographic and functional issues (e.g., low socioeconomic status, behavioral and academic problems) from kindergarten through first grade. Students placed at risk in kindergarten had different outcomes in first grade depending on the level of instructional and emotional support provided by their teacher. The academic achievement of students who received strong support was similar to that of low-risk students. In contrast, at-risk students had more conflicts with teachers and lower achievement in less supportive classrooms (with teachers who were less warm, responsive, sensitive, etc.).

Effective classroom management is an important component of the supportive classroom, and it is aligned with the idea of proactive classroom management. A proactive classroom manager is a teacher who creates opportunities for students to behave as expected, then reinforces with praise for desirable behaviors and positively redirects misbehavior before the classroom is disrupted. To illustrate, the dramatic differences my colleagues and I (Bohn, Roehrig, and Pressley 2004) observed in different teachers' classrooms at the beginning of the year were followed by starkly different student outcomes when we visited them again later in the school year. The students whose teachers had spent more time on developing classroom rules and routines tended to write more and independently apply reading strategies, participated in learning activities with excitement, and expressed desire to participate in discussions and read new books. Less time was lost disciplining students because students knew the expectations and did not require repeated reminders of the procedures. The conclusion: establishing students' self-regulation for behavior and learning can help you and students make the most of the time you have together. (Note that although establishing routines is a focus of the beginning of the year, routines also should be revisited throughout the year. Beth and I will emphasize in Section 3 that it is important to reinforce and model procedures throughout the school year.)

For examples of reinforcing and modeling procedures

see Section 3, page 56

There are opportunities during productive noninstructional time for you to make the morning welcome support your students' focus and attitudes about learning, ways to make transitions efficient and supportive of students' ability to self-regulate (the process of "regulating one's thinking, emotions and behavior" [Florez 2011, 46]), as well as ways to enhance students' ownership of their classroom community and learning during clean-up at the end of the day. Beth and I will provide some practical suggestions on how to do this in Section 3.

How Does Reactive Classroom Management Lose Time?

There is much research to support that reactive classroom management strategies, which can lead to distractions and interruptions, may negatively impact use of time and ultimately achievement (e.g., Freiberg, Stein, and Huang 1995; Hamre and Pianta 2005; Wasson, Beare, and Wasson 1990). My colleagues and I (Bohn, Roehrig, and Pressley 2004) found that teachers whose students were not very engaged later in the school year focused on instruction regardless of whether students were off task, tended to use preset rules without enlisting much student help with creating them, and threatened students with punishment. If they used modeling at all it was usually to make negative models of children who were doing behaviors the teachers did not like by pointing out their "mistakes" to the rest of the class. During the first couple days of school, these teachers spent most of students' time on content instruction. Because little time was devoted to making the expectations and procedures clear in positive ways, instructional time was repeatedly interrupted by the teacher reminding students about procedures. In other words, the absence of productive noninstructional time led to lost instructional time. Teachers lost time disciplining their students because students didn't "know what they [were] supposed to be doing" (Bohn, Roehrig, and Pressley 2004, 270). Their students also expressed disinterest with learning activities, often failed to do their homework, used reading strategies less independently, and had less impressive reading and writing achievement.

Clear Expectations and Practice of Procedures

Proactive classroom management techniques that emphasize clear expectations and practice of procedures at the beginning of the year (even with continuous monitoring and reteaching as needed throughout the year) save time over the course of the school year (Simonsen et al. 2008; Smith 2000). Specifically, proactive classroom management techniques reduce the amount of time wasted on reactive classroom management that can distract you and your students from learning. Students need a classroom management framework to support the use of instructional time. The wisdom in devoting time to this is supported by other research on elementary grades (Emmer, Evertson, and Anderson 1980) and secondary grades (Evertson and Emmer 1982). The work of Emmer and Evertson, especially about the beginning of the school year, has been the basis of numerous popular classroom management textbooks. Setting up routine procedures during the first couple weeks of school for everything from turning in papers to sharpening pencils, monitoring students closely, and stopping inappropriate behaviors immediately is positively related to lower rates of off-task behavior and higher rates of student engagement and achievement later in the school year (Emmer, Evertson, and Anderson 1980).

For example, Brooks (1985) videotaped activities in the classrooms of four secondary schoolteachers on their first days of school. When he analyzed the recordings, he found that the less experienced teachers tended to spend little time on expectations and procedures. Teachers who provided more opportunity for learning the rules and procedures were perceived as clearer and better prepared by students and had fewer student behavior/management problems. Indeed, numerous studies support the effectiveness of "post, teach, review, monitor, and reinforce expectations" (Simonsen et al. 2008, 354). More specifically,

> *Posting, teaching, and reviewing expectations* (i.e., social skills) and providing feedback are associated with (a) decreases in off-task behavior and disruptive behavior (i.e., talking out) and (b) increases in academic engagement, leadership, and conflict resolution. (Simonsen et al. 2008, 358)

In Section 3, you'll learn the how-to, but for some research-based classroom management strategies that promote students' academic motivation and self-regulation, see Figure 2–5.

Figure 2–5 Classroom Management Strategies That Support Students' Motivation and Self-Regulation

1. The teacher constantly assesses students' engagement, understanding, and behavior throughout the day.

2. The teacher has rules, procedures, policies, and routines for students that are useful and provide smooth transitions within lessons and between activities.

3. The teacher has provided ways for students to monitor their learning and transition independently to some activities after they are finished.

4. The students are given responsibilities to help maintain the cleanliness and orderliness of their classroom.

5. The teacher clearly communicates expectations for student behavior and learning.

6. The teacher and students discuss the reasons behind activities, rules, procedures, and routines.

7. The teacher provides extrinsic rewards for appropriate behaviors and activities not as bribes but to extend learning; rewards that produce learning (e.g., an opportunity to do some free reading) are used.

8. The teacher uses classroom management techniques that are positive, constructive, and encouraging toward students.

9. When students are disciplined for their behaviors, the punishment is a natural consequence for the transgression.

Adapted from Tables 2.1 and 2.4 in Pressley, Dolezal et al. (2003)

Classroom Community

The research evidence is quite clear: building a classroom community is not a time waster! The quality of relationships that students form with their teachers and peers is related to better social, emotional, and academic outcomes (for a review, see Watson and Battistich 2006). This is addressed extensively in *No More Taking Away Recess and Other Problematic Disciplinary Practices* (Cassetta and Sawyer 2013). But it is so important that it bears repeating: a classroom should be an authentic, caring, respectful community that is supportive, but not controlling, and focused on learning. Some ways to support such a community include greeting your students by name at the door each morning and taking time to talk to each of your students personally during the week. The Responsive Classroom approach is one well-researched program (for a review of the evidence, see McTigue and Rimm-Kaufman [2010]) with strategies to help you build such a community. (You can learn more about the Responsive Classroom approach and the research behind it at www.responsiveclassroom.org.)

Not Just a One-Time Investment

There is little in the research to suggest how much is the right amount of time to spend on establishing and maintaining routines and classroom community during the school year, as it likely depends on both you and your students and the school context. However, it is important to point out that effective teachers were observed to use such strategies later in the school year as well (Bohn, Roehrig, and Pressley 2004). To maintain the classroom management framework you have established at the beginning of the year, you need to monitor students' engagement and behavior, model or practice again as needed, and be consistent about providing specific praise, reminders, and appropriate consequences as needed.

Gettinger and Walter (2012) offer numerous suggestions for facilitating close monitoring, including seating arrangements that allow you to see behaviors from anywhere, spending less time at your desk, circulating around the room frequently, and using student volunteers to hand out materials. Active supervision and precorrection also can improve transition behavior (Colvin et al. 1997). Thus, it is important not only to focus on establishing community and teaching expectations and procedures early in the school year, but also to continue paying attention to these throughout the year. It is very likely that you'll identify new community topics and procedures you want to discuss, and students may need refreshers on familiar topics and procedures. See Figure 2–6 for some examples of research-based classroom atmosphere strategies that support students' motivation and self-regulation.

Figure 2–6   Classroom Atmosphere Strategies That Support Students' Motivation and Self-Regulation

1. The classroom is filled with books at different reading levels for students to use.

2. The teacher has high expectations that students are aware of.

3. The teacher and students work together to create and accomplish learning tasks.

4. The teacher communicates to students that he believes students can learn and be successful with challenging activities.

5. The teacher creates an atmosphere of warmth, care, and concern for students by interacting with students in a caring way, using humor in a positive way, expressing positive attitudes toward all students, and so on.

6. The teacher creates a community of learners in the classroom.

7. Students are given choices.

8. The teacher models enthusiasm for learning and provides activities that pique students' curiosity.

9. The teacher takes advantage of many opportunities to give constructive feedback to students that is immediate and specific to their accomplishments.

Adapted from Table 2.1 in Pressley, Dolezal et al. (2003)

Instructional Strategies

If there are behavior problems, it is hard to provide good instruction, but keeping students engaged in instruction is a good way to keep them from misbehaving (Roehrig et al. 2012). We have probably all observed or experienced lessons (as a teacher or student) like the ones Beth described in Section 1—Ms. June and Mr. Gillis did not plan their instructional activities to meet their intended learning objectives and assessments. As a result, Phoebe and Luke participated in the fun, hands-on activities, but they did not get much meaningful learning out of them. Ms. Barry also struggled with this. She relied too much on spontaneous instruction, and as a result Roberta felt lost and she certainly wasn't engaged. What they all ended up with was unproductive instructional time. They lacked what my colleagues and I have observed in the elementary classrooms with the students who are highly engaged and evidencing high levels of achievement in their work: instructional density. I and others have described instructional density (Wharton-McDonald, Pressley, and Hampston 1998)—the teachers and students within the class are always engaged in learning opportunities so rich and plentiful that I have trouble capturing all that is going on in my notes! (See Figure 2–7 for key characteristics of instructional density summarized by Pressley, Roehrig et al. [2003].)

Poor Instructional Planning Leads to Lost Learning

How does a teacher achieve such density? It is likely that planning plays a huge role in supporting the efficient use of time to address multiple objectives in an individualized fashion nonstop throughout a school day. There is little research, however, on the effects of teachers' planning (or lack thereof) per se on their use of time and ultimately students' engagement and learning. It is hard to study planning without stimulating teachers to plan to some degree, and there can be a profound gap between the intentions captured in a plan and how it is implemented in the classroom. However, potential benefits of planning can be seen in the findings of Connor and her colleagues (2009) as well as the work of the Fuchses and their colleagues (Fuchs et al. 1991). Both teams of researchers have found that student achievement

Figure 2–7   Characteristics of Instructional Density

- Teacher highly organized to implement many well-planned learning opportunities
- Multiple instructional groupings used throughout the day (e.g., different small groups implemented—not just whole-class instruction)
- Multiple instructional strategies used throughout the day (e.g., demonstrations, explanations, discussions, hands-on activities, etc.—not just worksheets or lecture)
- More time and attention spent on academically rigorous activities (e.g., writing rather than illustrating)
- Teachable moments taken advantage of by teacher (e.g., teacher notices students are struggling with a relevant skill and takes time to teach or reinforce the teaching of that skill)
- Students not allowed to be idle during instructional time

(Pressley, Roehrig et al. 2003)

was lower when the teachers were not carefully implementing individualized instruction they planned based on student assessment data. The work of Connor and Fuchs and their colleagues have in common the use of student assessment data to drive instructional planning, and supports for instructional implementation (like coaches and software) were also found to be immensely helpful.

Assessment

Teachers often tell me about the hours and hours they spend practicing for, administering, and scoring assessments. Don't even get me going on the amount of time teachers in some states spend on practicing for high-stakes tests (e.g., more than 20 percent of their time in North Carolina; for a review of assessment and student engagement, see Nichols and Dawson [2012]). I understand how this can feel like a huge waste of time—you could be doing more engaging instruction instead of dealing with these assessments! There is some room, however, to make your administration and scoring of assessments much more efficient using technology. Although some of the new tools (e.g., computer programs, web-based assessments, handheld devices, and student response systems) admittedly take a lot of your nonclassroom time to learn and master, I think it is worth it in the long run because of how powerful assessment can be.

In particular, the results of formative assessment can help to enhance students' engagement and learning, thus making the use of instructional time more productive (Bennett 2011; Nichols and Dawson 2012), and even help you to be successful with classroom management (see Figure 2–5). Using technologies, such as those in Figure 2–8, can help you to save time on the back end in terms of less time to evaluate students' response or enter student data. Plus, obtaining real-time data on student understanding can help to enhance the quality of the instructional time by facilitating immediate and specific feedback (Shute 2008) and give you the information you need to modify your instruction (e.g., reteach a concept students are struggling with). Teachers should constantly assess students' engagement, understanding, and behavior throughout the day (Wharton-McDonald, Pressley, and Hampston 1998).

Teachers need to be careful, however, about how they allow assessments to affect their instruction. As I mentioned earlier, much time may be wasted on high-stakes test practice. And I suspect that such practice may not even provide appropriate learning opportunities to support the objectives that the tests are intended to measure. Spending much of your time (especially as the date of the big test draws near) talking about and teaching to the test rather than the learning objectives are potential time traps that teachers can get sucked into (Shepard and Dougherty 1991). These are examples of unproductive instructional time that don't even result in transfer of learning to other tests (Amrein and Berliner 2002). Such strategies can backfire by vir-

Figure 2–8 Examples of Assessment Technology

Electronic personal response systems or clickers

- Students "click" to provide immediate private responses to assessments or polls.
- Teachers can get immediate summaries of responses that can be shared with students and used to immediately address misunderstandings.

Web-based progress monitoring or curriculum-based measures

- Students complete individual assessments on a computer in a computer lab or during centers.
- Teachers can work with other students while the program tallies scores and uploads results.

Personal digital assistants or handheld devices

- Evaluations of individual student responses are immediately entered by the teacher.
- The device can tally scores and upload results, minimizing paperwork and errors.

tue of inhibiting deep learning and being demotivating (again, for a powerful review about the relationship between testing and student engagement, see Nichols and Dawson [2012]). Research on effective teaching practices and teachers tells us that the best ways to improve student learning outcomes are through feedback and remediation, establishing appropriately challenging goals and a supportive classroom environment, and focusing on mastery learning (e.g., Hughes, Wu, and West 2011) rather than performance (for a review see Hattie [2003]). At least at the secondary school level, research suggests that in higher-performing schools (as compared to schools with more typical student achievement outcomes) teachers did not treat test prep as separate from the curriculum; rather, instruction and practice related to the outcomes to be tested were integrated into the regular daily instruction (Langer 2001).

Rather than teaching to the test, it is important to focus on learning deeply for the sake of learning and applying that knowledge to real problems, rather than just to pass a test (Smith and Rottenberg 2005). Most big state tests, and the ones being developed for the new Common Core State Standards, are designed to assess particular objectives. If you put your energy into planning your instruction to meet the objectives (to enhance productive instructional time), rather than into spending lots of time taking practice tests, your students should find that the high-stakes tests measure the minimum competencies that you set for your students. In so doing, you may also help to alleviate some of the rampant anxiety students often have about such exams (McDonald 2001).

Instructional Routines and Procedures

Teaching and practicing instructional routines and procedures can help you to be sure that students understand what they are supposed to be doing and actually do it, which benefits classroom management, too. Routines that involve even low-tech student response techniques (e.g., having students hold up index cards or hand signals to display their answer choice or level of understanding) can help reduce disruptive behavior (Armendariz and Umbreit 1999) and improve students' motivation and engagement in learning. Armendariz and Umbreit used paper response cards, though this could easily be adapted for use with electronic response systems like clickers (see Figure 2–8). Instructional routines are also embedded in research-based instructional programs and methods such as CORI (described under Relevance and Choice) and reciprocal teaching (Palincsar and Brown 1984), which also both support students' self-regulation. In reciprocal teaching, the procedures focus on teachers' scaffolding and gradual release of students' application of reading comprehension strategies in small cooperative groups (Palincsar and Brown 1984; Rosenshine and Meister 1994). Indeed, Palincsar (2007) has emphasized the central role of dialogue in the process of students "trying on and becoming proficient in the use of these strategies" (43) during reciprocal teaching.

Relevance and Choice

Allowing students opportunities to make choices is associated with creating a motivating classroom atmosphere (see Figure 2–6), but perhaps because of that it is also an important component of motivating classroom instruction. Choice can be powerful because it supports students' sense of autonomy (control) while also increasing the probability that the learning task or content will be more relevant to each student. It is not advisable to let students decide to do (or *not* do) whatever they want with little constraint—classroom chaos, frustrated students, and less learning would likely ensue. But offering students choices from a carefully considered set of options is very important. For example, you can give students a choice of whether to read about either Asia, Africa, or Europe when you offer them a choice of books (all at their independent reading level) to read for a social studies project related to societies on the different continents.

Relevance and choice have also been systematically leveraged in research-based curricula for teaching reading and science. For instance, Guthrie and his colleagues designed Concept Oriented Reading Instruction (CORI; Guthrie et al. 2004) to saturate literacy and science inquiry with strategies to help make learning relevant for students. CORI is an example of a powerful instructional method that focuses on deep learning and making connections between subject areas, while efficiently covering objectives in both science and reading. It also includes cooperative learning groups and collaborative activities. CORI has been shown to increase students' reading engagement, motivation, and comprehension (Guthrie et al. 2004; Wigfield et al. 2008). This program is so successful at improving students' engagement and achievement in part because it is based on theories of motivation and self-regulation:

In CORI, teachers implement the following practices over a 12-week period in language arts blocks of 90–120 minutes per day: (a) using concept goals in a conceptual theme for reading instruction, (b) affording choices and control to students, (c) providing hands-on activities related to the content goals, (d) using interesting texts of diverse genre for instruction, and (e) organizing collaboration for learning from all texts. (Guthrie et al. 2004, 11–12)

Specific Praise and Feedback

Providing timely, specific, and constructive feedback is not only associated with creating a motivating classroom atmosphere (see Figure 2–6). Specific praise has been found to improve students' on-task behavior as well as their enjoyment of lessons about numeracy (Chalk and Bizo 2004). Specific praise means you go beyond a generic "Good job!" to include details about improvements, effort, mastery, accuracy, and so on by adding something like, "I noticed you identified and corrected three mistakes in your journal today. Your time and effort proofreading has paid off! Your work shows you have mastered this (specific) writing standard." In their study, Chalk and Bizo (2004) also point out the role of specific praise or feedback in the development of self-regulated learning (SRL):

> SRL is developed in classrooms by providing timely, informative, and encouraging private feedback rather than public comparison of performance . . . and through encouraging pupil[s] to reflect on learning. . . . Specific praise could increase a learner's knowledge of the learning strategies and effort required for success, thus increasing SRL. (338)

Beyond the general attributes of effective feedback outlined above, it is also important to note that characteristics of both the learning task and the learner can impact how well different sorts of feedback promote learning (see Figure 2–9).

Figure 2–9 Formative Feedback Guidelines

In general do . . .

- focus feedback on the task, not the learner.

- present elaborated feedback in manageable units.

- be specific and clear with feedback message.

- give unbiased, objective feedback, written or via computer.

- use "praise" sparingly, if at all.

- avoid using progressive hints that always terminate with the correct answer (consider using more specific prompts and cues instead).

- not present feedback that discourages the learner, threatens the learner's self-esteem, or is too controlling or critical of the learner.

- not interrupt learner with feedback if the learner is actively engaged.

Use delayed feedback for . . .

- relatively simple tasks.

- promoting transfer of learning.

- high-achieving learners.

Use immediate feedback for . . .

- difficult tasks.

- retention of procedural or conceptual knowledge.

- low-achieving learners.

For low-achieving learners use . . .

- directive or corrective feedback to provide more explicit guidance.

- scaffolding (more early support and structure).

For high-achieving learners use . . .

- facilitative feedback that challenges them.

- verification feedback that allows them to proceed at their own pace.

Adapted from Tables 2–5 in Shute (2008)

Matching Instruction to Students' Performance Level

I have already discussed research supporting the importance of matching instruction to students' present performance level (Connor et al. 2007, 2009), and others have noted this strategy as well (e.g., Gettinger and Walter 2012). Teachers should provide appropriately challenging activities in students' ZPD and provide scaffolding (Cheyne and Tarulli 1999). Guided by students' ZPD, this match forms the basis of the effective use of the time students spend working independently (when the tasks should not be too difficult that the individual alone cannot complete it), in small groups of students (the challenge level should be that which an individual student could achieve with the support of group members), and the time you spend working one-on-one with individuals (when the tasks should be even a little more difficult). Keep in mind, however, that tasks that are too easy can be just as demotivating as tasks that are too hard (Locke and Latham 2002).

Matching instruction to students' abilities has other benefits as well. When teachers have individualized, meaningful instructional conversations with students in their ZPD, they can build the quality of their relationships with one another in ways that increase students' engagement (Tharp et al. 2000). Moreover, when your actions help students to know you care about their needs and you are willing to work with them to meet your high expectations, the positive tone of the classroom atmosphere is also reinforced (see Figure 2–6).

Quality Tasks

Of course the quality of the task you want students to spend time on (and of their cognitive processing while performing that task) matters too. For example, you may plan a high-quality instructional opportunity (targeted to a science literacy objective) for your fourth graders. You ask students to apply self-questioning strategies (e.g., What problem needs investigating? What do we already know?) in small-group discussions after reading a science text. This type of activity has been shown to improve fourth-grade students' metacognitive awareness and science learning (Michalsky, Mevarach, and Haibi 2013). But what if your students are not cognitively engaged while completing the task? Were they sufficiently motivated to participate in the task? Did they give up and go off task when they got distracted by something else going on in the classroom or got frustrated with some part of the activity? Did you help the students come up with a purpose for the learning that matched the objective and also had relevance for the student? John Guthrie (2001), a well-regarded researcher who focuses on motivating instruction, put it best: "Without the presence of cognitive and motivational dimensions together, engagement cannot occur" (sec. Strategy Instruction). Just making more time for instruction is clearly *not* sufficient! Figure 2–10 provides a summary of some research-based instructional strategies to support students' academic motivation. A brief introduction to these has been provided here in Section 2, but you'll learn more about making instruction engaging in Section 3.

Student Engagement Is a Reflection of Teacher Actions

I began this section with the idea that less effective teachers do not believe student engagement is within their control. The goal of this section was to provide credible evidence that it is and that engagement is the most important indicator of effective instructional time. When we observed six primary-grade teachers at the beginning of the year and then later in the school year, my colleagues and I were amazed by what we saw (Bohn, Roehrig, and Pressley 2004). Teachers with high and low levels of student engagement started the school year in dramatically different ways and maintained those behaviors throughout the year—the more effective teachers' practices were saturated with many of the behaviors I have touched on throughout this section. You may have noticed some overlap between strategies presented in Figures 2–5, 2–6, and 2–10, which makes sense given the mutually reinforcing nature of teachers' classroom management, atmosphere, and

Figure 2–10 Instructional Strategies That Support Students' Motivation and Self-Regulation

1. The teacher gives clear directions in a precise, easy-to-follow way, checking for understanding as each step is completed.

2. The teacher checks for and monitors students' understanding of the material. She probes for answers, allows wait time for students to think before answering, and encourages them to self-correct their wrong answers.

3. The teacher provides activities and lessons that promote deep processing and higher-order thinking skills.

4. To teach a single concept, the teacher uses many different methods to deliver the lesson's content.

5. The teacher makes connections across lessons/activities and connects what is being learned to the outside world.

6. Lessons are organized and well planned; there is little downtime between activities.

7. The teacher talks aloud, modeling thought processes while demonstrating activities and strategies for students.

8. The teacher provides explicit instruction of strategies.

9. The teacher provides appropriately challenging activities in students' ZPD and provides scaffolding.

10. The teacher uses cooperative learning strategies.

Adapted from Table 2.1 in Pressley, Dolezal et al. (2003)

instructional practices for developing and sustaining students' motivation and self-regulation (Roehrig et al. 2012). See Figure 2–11 for a quick overview of some of the most salient actions effective teachers took to foster student engagement.

Figure 2–11 **Teacher Actions That Foster Student Engagement**

- Spend time stressing community values.

- Consistently express high, positive expectations.

- Give students input on creating classroom rules.

- Explain, model, and practice procedures.

- Encourage students to perform routines independently and to be reflective and monitor their own behaviors by asking them to think about how to do something before asking for help.

Now, just imagine how very different those student stories in Section 1 might have been if the teachers had employed these sorts of strategies!

SECTION 3

BUT THAT

How to Maximize Academic Engaged Time

ELIZABETH H. BRINKERHOFF AND **ALYSIA D. ROEHRIG**

We struggled a bit as we thought about how to write this section. Sometimes, professional development sounds like an angry sermon. The anger usually comes from a sense of urgency, a desire to help kids and teachers. It's not conscious malice, but it does communicate a lack of respect and faith in one's audience. Although we live in a climate of teacher bashing, we don't ascribe to it. We know better because we've seen too many great teachers in action. So before we get into the nitty-gritty of practice, we want to acknowledge that you might be doing many of the practices in this section already and that you might also have great ideas that we've never heard of. But we're putting this information out there because we know too many teachers who have had to figure this out on their own. That was a waste of their and their students' time! Even if you know you already use your students' time well, it can be helpful to have an articulated framework with research citations to back you up. And maybe seeing all the practices brought together will give you ideas for some improvements you can make. That's what makes teaching a great, albeit sometimes frustrating, profession: there's always room for improvement.

So let's take a moment to return to the time evaluation tools from Section 1. In Section 2, Alysia introduced a phrase to describe the most valuable kind of time in your classroom—*academic engaged time*—as the time students are actively doing the cognitive processes that matter to learning. While doing so, students are motivated to persevere through self-regulated decision-making opportunities. For our students to get as much out of their time with us as we have to give, we need to measure and maximize academic engaged time. In Section 1, Beth asked you to evaluate your time by comparing what actually happened to what was planned and how students behaved during that time. How did you do? Were there some uses of time that surprised you? Some that pleased you? Some that startled you? And to get more concrete, do students spend more time listening to you than doing what they need to grow as learners? It's worth revisiting the evaluation tools in Section 1 to reflect on how the research Alysia presented in Section 2 has clarified or informed your thinking. It may also help you decide which practices you want to prioritize in this section (see Figure 3–1).

Figure 3–1   Note from Beth

> Where do I begin? For me, that is exactly what I am thinking about as I return to the elementary classroom after a two-year leave of absence. I know I'll be mindful of these practices at the beginning of the school year. But, if I were in the middle of the school year, I would be using the same process for salvaging valuable time. If I remember that academic engaged time is about quantity and quality—we start with a moment and we add to it—both time and depth of teaching—then I give myself permission to start wherever I am.
>
> —Beth

Where Do We Begin?

We can begin by thinking about the three elements that Alysia explained in Section 2—engaging every learner, productive noninstructional time, and productive instructional time. These collaboratively enhance the quantity and quality of academic engaged time (see Figure 3–2).

As the figure demonstrates, these three elements reinforce one another. So it's good to know that you can begin anywhere. If you're in the middle of the school year, you might go for the low-hanging fruit first. What's something that feels doable to you right now? Progress in one area will facilitate progress in the others reciprocally (and provide you with a feeling of empowerment). For example, you could design the morning welcome to support your students' focus and attitudes about learning, make transitions efficient and supportive of students' ability to self-regulate, or enhance students' ownership of their classroom community and learning during clean-up at the end of the day (all productive uses of noninstructional time; see Appendix A for

Figure 3–2 Maximized Academic Engaged Time

ENGAGING LEARNERS
To support students' self-regulation of learning and behavior:

- Have students set down learning goals.
- Incorporate self-monitoring procedures.
- Teach students to use metacognitive learning strategies.

Increase quality of learning activities

PRODUCTIVE INSTRUCTIONAL TIME
To support smooth delivery of instruction at efficient pace:

- Make learning relevant.
- Provide frequent feedback.
- Match instruction to clear objectives and students' abilities.

Increase student engagement

Increase instructional time

PRODUCTIVE NONINSTRUCTIONAL TIME
To reduce transition times and minimize disruptions and off-task behavior:

- Build classroom community.
- Establish efficient routines.

resources on these practices). So, although this section unfolds in a specific sequence, you are the one teaching your students right now. Take from this section what you need.

You'll see that Section 3 is organized around student understandings and behaviors—these are the ways we can assess the use of our time. For example, are students able to explain why the classroom rules are important and follow them? Do students appear to be enthusiastically engaged in learning activities and not get distracted? (See some tools for observing and evaluating your students' engagement under Assessment tools in Appendix A.) We begin the section by describing what happens when you make good use of noninstructional time; then, we focus on instructional time. Strategies for engaging learners are incorporated throughout all our suggestions on how you might use both types of time.

Productive Noninstructional Time: Go Team!

One of the first things to recognize is that students who are mutually respectful and supportive are better able to work through differences for the sake of learning. We might think of our class as a team working together as a learning community. Building the class as a team (or family) and developing teamwork within small groups are both important. As Alysia pointed out in Section 2, there is research that supports building the classroom community, and different authors offer a multitude of opinions on how this should be done. As suggested by Frey and Fisher (2011), Beth personally attempts to facilitate a teamlike cohesiveness between students and between students and herself. And, we agree, students in the elementary classroom, just like a winning team, must work together toward a common goal or purpose. See Figure 3–3 for ideas for using noninstructional time for developing a teamlike environment. In this environment, less time is wasted on lack of focus or clarity.

Figure 3–3   Steps to Developing Classroom Environment

Using the "team" idea as a framework, list the qualities that you and your students need to have to play on the same team.

- Goal for class

- Strong communication that is both respectful and productive for the goal

- Supportive, caring relationships between teacher and students

- An understanding of peers' strengths and weaknesses (useful for collaboration also)

- An understanding of classroom procedures that help to facilitate learning

Next, create an action plan that involves all of the members of the class. Your plan may include:

- Discussion of why you are at school (purpose)

- Building communication skills using routines as frames during interaction (For example, you may provide the sentence "My favorite thing about school is _____, but I really don't like _____.") In time, students won't need the framing sentence, but initially this may be helpful.

Whose Behavioral Expectations Are They?

All teams have rules: a set of behavioral expectations for playing on the team. Because the students are going to need to abide by the team rules, they can share in the responsibility for developing their team's behavioral expectations (i.e., rules). Using the guidelines from the Responsive Classroom approach, students can develop the expectations that will govern the team (class). (See Figure 3–4 for tips on how to establish team expectations with your students.) This gives them little excuse for lack of buy-in, and you can go a step further and have them establish the consequences for lack of adherence to the agreed upon expectations.

Figure 3–4   Establishing Team Expectations with Your Class

Consistent with self-regulation, students can, in collaboration with the teacher and other students, develop the rules that they will follow. The Responsive Classroom website (responsiveclassroom .org) offers suggestions for the beginning of the school year. Working with students to come to consensus on a common purpose in the classroom community environment is key to successfully engaging students in developing their own governance structure and behavioral expectations.

Students Know What's Expected of Them and Do It on Their Own

A professional development instructor once said, "If you don't teach students what you expect, they will make it up, and you won't like it." We couldn't agree more! Beyond rules, there also are procedures that students participate in daily such as caring for supplies, storing personal items, and preparing for transition. You should not assume that students know the procedures you would like them to use for going to the bathroom and sharpening their pencils. Such procedures may appear rigid at first, but they are sensible in that they allow you to not waste time on menial tasks like pencil sharpening. You set up these basics so that students can move on to more important tasks. You will modify these seemingly rigid procedures over time, and hopefully you will be able to do this collaboratively with your students so that they remain empowered and self-regulated.

Other things that you need to consider are transitions and maintenance of the expectations during the school year. You can lose time on transitions, so you will need to look at your boundaries and resources. (See Appendix B for a collection of transition ideas.) You will also need to decide how you are planning to maintain the desired procedures. Chances are, if you practice them early in the process (or early in the school year if you are able to start at the beginning), you will need minimal maintenance. Because students will understand each procedure

Figure 3–5 Return to Charles' Story

> Remember Charles in Ms. Ford's class? He was bewildered when the teacher called his dad at work. Charles didn't know the procedure for obtaining help, so he made it up. She didn't like it. He was in trouble, but really, he would have complied if he had known the procedure for getting help.

and its benefits, they will be more likely to value it. To illustrate, let's return briefly to Charles' story from Section 1 in Figure 3–5.

Here's the thing: our own understanding of our expectations might be a bit hazy. If we've never forced ourselves to articulate them, then it's worth doing so. We tell students how important writing and talking are as thinking tools; we might as well use them ourselves. Take some time alone to write down the actions your students need to take during the course of a day. You might look back to the time evaluation tool to pinpoint some opportunities to clarify expectations. You might not even need the evaluation tool to know where to begin. Sometimes, our own irritation/frustration is an adequate indicator that we need to rethink how we're spending our time. For some help describing the procedure, follow the planning steps in Figure 3–6. You'll find a helpful acronym, CHAMP, which outlines five aspects of each procedure when deciding how to teach for understanding and clarity (Sprick, Garrison, and Howard 1998).

Beyond establishing rules, procedures, community, and so on, which all lead to proactive classroom management, there comes a time when reactive responses are needed for some students. One way to continue with the teamlike relationships that you are building is to have students provide guidance for the consequences they will expect (except in extreme cases). An example from Beth's own second-grade classroom experience is provided in Figure 3–7.

Figure 3–6 Planning Steps for Procedural Routines

Use CHAMP: A Tool for Planning and Describing Procedural Routines

Conversation: Can students talk to each other? When? How loud? To whom?

Help: What do students do if they need help? Who and how do they ask?

Activity: Exactly what will students do? What will the end product look like?

Movement: What type of movement is permitted? What will the movement look like?

Participation: What does the students' behavior look like while they are participating?

Most daily tasks can be made more efficient by procedural routines.

After you've described the routines of one day, consider procedures that may be hidden within the procedures listed such as the quiet signal, movement in the classroom, and so on.

Plan instruction, modeling, and practice (ideally, during the first week of school, but better late than never).

If you can find a colleague to partner with, talk through the procedures with him or her to test your clarity. Discuss why this procedural routine is important. Be prepared to give your students a rationale. Students are more likely to comply if you give them a reason. Talking through each procedure will help you to polish the procedure prior to teaching your students.

Consider what practice may be needed for maintaining the procedure. Make sure you let students know when they're doing well and when they've mastered it.

Figure 3–7   Students Can Provide Guidance for Consequences

I have asked students what they thought should happen when someone didn't follow the rules they had established, and students were actually much harder on themselves and their peers than I was comfortable with. They had good ideas, however, that I was able to tweak into the consequences they still viewed as their own. For example, for years I have used a monetary system (Brinkerhoff Bucks—my picture on the bucks and everything) for teaching students practical use of mathematics in real life. Students pay rent, go shopping on Friday from the class store, and use their bucks to access other privileges. One group of students decided that I should take all of the offender's bucks for the week upon failure to follow the rules the class had created, and I reduced it to paying a $5 fine. This was acceptable to the students, especially since we had recently viewed a film clip of what it means to be a good citizen. In the film, offenders paid a fine . . . great connection between the mathematics curriculum, self-regulation (choice of rules and consequences), and classroom management!

—Beth

(For more on how to enact proactive classroom management, see *No More Taking Away Recess and Other Problematic Disciplinary Practices* by Cassetta and Sawyer [2013] on this topic.)

Students Respect Others Because They Are Respected

If we only talked about procedural routines as a time-saver, then we'd risk reinforcing the factory model of school. We'd be building something without a strong enough foundation to withstand the natural adversity of human beings. Students need positive social relationships with their peers and you: "Children learn best when they have both academic and social-emotional skills" (Casto and Audley 2008, 11). When we feel like we are part of a community, we are more motivated to behave in socially desirable ways (which could reinforce positive classroom management) and we are more likely to take risks and not worry about failing (which could support the learning motivation and effort of our students).

Morning meeting is a routine for establishing community and a mutual appreciation for others. Beginning each day with a greeting, sharing, an activity, and the class news helps your students to build social skills and learn to cooperate with others. (See Figure 3–8 for the elements of morning meeting.) Morning meeting is a time for developing the relationships needed in a classroom community. It begins with a daily greeting. The greeting reinforces the need for respectfully responding to every student in the community. In addition, the second component, sharing, provides the opportunity for students to recognize the life experiences they have in common and to identify areas where others in their community have needs that the classroom as a community may help to meet. The daily activity or game during the morning meeting offers a time for play, conversation, and fun. Most of all, students have their blood and their brain active simultaneously. They are ready for the news and learning the purpose of learning for the day.

Figure 3–8 Morning Meeting Design

1. Begins with a greeting (reinforces the need to respond respectfully to every student in the community): 2 minutes

2. Sharing personal experiences (provides the opportunity for students to recognize the life experiences they have in common and highlights strengths and needs of others): 5 minutes

3. Activity (a time for play, fun, conversation): 5 minutes

4. News and purpose for learning for the given day: 3 minutes

Note about time management: The morning meeting is designed to launch the day. Some teachers unintentionally fall into the habit of marathon meetings. The meeting should last from 10–15 minutes, and each activity within it should be carefully analyzed and monitored to ensure that it is worthy of the time spent. This helps to maintain instructional momentum in the day.

Within the framework of morning meeting, conflict can be addressed as the need arises. For example, you learn of a situation where one student has been bullying another student, and within the greeting, sharing, activity, and news, you are able to build in a character lesson and enlist the other students in the class to help eliminate the problem behavior. You will spend less time responding to frequent student conflicts. From experience, we know that the "time one commits to Morning Meeting is an investment which is repaid many times over . . . Morning Meeting is a microcosm of the way we wish our schools to be—communities full of learning, safe and respectful and challenging for all" (Kriete and Bechtel 2002, 3).

How do we define "engagement"?

see Section 2, page 21

Remember Ms. Ford from Section 1? Fast forward one year. Ms. Ford recognizes the need for students to become self-regulated learners, and with this in mind, she builds an atmosphere where procedures are understood by all and students can eventually monitor their learning and behavior (with teacher scaffolding) to make appropriate decisions during the school day (with fewer and fewer reminders). As students arrive on the first day of school, she greets each one at the door and directs them toward their seats, saying quietly, "After you put your folder and backpack away, go to your seat, and read the note on the board." This allows her to facilitate a quiet, personable entrance into the room. Then, she points out that there will be a note on the board each day when they enter the room. The note will give them an idea of what they will be doing on that day. She probes for their understanding by saying, "What will you learn today?" A few children raise their hands, and they all agree that they will be learning procedures on the first day of school. Ms. Ford probes further, "Think for just a minute. No talking, just thinking. What are procedures?" After about thirty seconds, Ms. Ford says, "Turn to your neighbor and tell them what you think procedures are." She allows about thirty seconds of sharing, and then, she says, "Give me your attention. Raise your hand if you think that you know what procedures are." Almost every hand is raised. Ms. Ford picks up a marker and writes the answers from her students on the board. As the year progresses, students learn procedures, and frequent reminders are unnecessary.

After recording a few of the students' answers, she tells the class that she will teach them the first procedure now. The first procedure is her quiet signal. Ms. Ford has selected "give me five" as her quiet signal. She explains that with this procedure, the person who is leading says, "Give me five" (see Figure 3–9). She points out that the quiet signal lets you know that the leader has something important to say (rationale). She continues by telling the students that the leader will often be the teacher, but there will be times when someone else, maybe one of the students, will be the leader. Ms. Ford practices the procedure slowly, following each step, reminding them of each step. She chooses a small group of students to assist in modeling this behavior. She directs the students to talk to each other about what they are going to do after school with a reminder that they should remember the procedure for "give me five." After about fifteen seconds of students' talking, Ms. Ford raises one hand and says, "Give me five." The students model the expected response by freezing in place, turning to look at Ms. Ford, becoming quiet and listening, emptying their hands, and raising one hand. Ms. Ford says to the class, "What did you see and hear?" Students raise their hands, and when she calls on them, they give their answers: "The kids each stopped talking," "They all put one hand up," "The students looked at you," and so on.

Figure 3–9 Procedural Routine: Quiet Signal

Ms. Ford explained, "The leader says, 'Give me five.' We do five things when the leader says this. First, we freeze where we are. Then, we turn and look at the leader. Third, we become silent so that we can hear the leader. Then, we empty our hands. Finally, we raise one hand so that the leader knows we are ready to hear what is said."

At this point, notice that Ms. Ford repeatedly provided the opportunity for students to reflect. In doing this, students not only had their attention drawn to important details, but they also received peer feedback. This helped students to begin the process of becoming self-regulated learners. Then, she had students practice this procedure several times in a similar fashion including asking students to comment on what they observed. When the students seemed to understand the procedure, Ms. Ford was ready to move on to learning other procedures. Introduction of this entire procedure only took the students a few minutes, but Ms. Ford now had a way to obtain her students' attention in an organized manner. During the next two weeks, students practiced "give me five." Ms. Ford realized that the students may need additional practice periodically, so she was already thinking of ways to build this practice into her instruction. More time used strategically!

Ms. Ford slowly and carefully progressed from behavior and procedural expectations in the hallway before school to the procedures for exiting the campus at the end of the day. She provided frequent modeling, time for reflection from students (sharing their observations), and practice for each procedure that she had identified in her planning. This process was tedious because of the amount of detail needed to be sure that students had a clear understanding of the procedures that they would use each day. (See Figure 3–10 for some common procedures to clarify with students.) The frequent interaction with their peers and their necessary participation in practicing the procedures kept students engaged. During the day, there were a few activities that the students did in addition to practicing the procedures, but these were housekeeping and getting to know your activities. The method of introduction, modeling, reflection, and practice of procedures provided Ms. Ford's class with a thorough understanding of what was expected of them in her class.

As her students learned to self-regulate their behavior and their learning, Ms. Ford turned over to students more and more of the

Figure 3–10 Possible Procedures to Clarify with Students

Possible procedures to clarify with students may include:

- care for and storage of materials

- morning entry

- what to do when there are needs (bathroom, questions, etc.)

- transitions

- and others.

responsibility for determining which procedures needed modification (or elimination), when and how procedures were to be practiced or reviewed, and when additional procedures or routines were needed to foster continued productive use of time. During the year, Ms. Ford built periodic review of these procedures into her lessons, and at the beginning of each quarter, she planned a complete review of all of the procedures, and she introduced new ones as needed. Whenever there appeared to be confusion about an expectation, Ms. Ford also reviewed the procedure, modeled the expectation, and required the students to reflect and practice. Thus, time that might have been wasted because of students' lack of understanding was available for uninterrupted instruction. Planning to teach procedural expectations takes time, but Ms. Ford could already see how the positive impact would enable her to make the best use of her instructional time.

Ms. Ford was thoughtful about teaching and reviewing expectations, but let's note something significant that she didn't do. Her expectations and rules were not just a bunch of don'ts. To be effective, teachers need to suggest desirable alternative behaviors. Students who are developing rules collaboratively with you may offer you don'ts, but craftily, you can transform them together through discussion into "do" statements. See some examples of collaboratively developed rule lists from Beth's second-grade classroom experience in Figure 3–11.

Figure 3–11 Rules for Two Different Years

Here are two lists of rules my students and I developed during two different school years. The rules vary from year to year, but essentially they represent the same desired behaviors. —Beth

One Year

1. Follow directions the first time.

2. Move carefully in the classroom.

3. Take care of supplies.

4. Respect every person.

Another Year

1. Keep my hands, feet, and all objects to myself.

2. Use my signal to tell the teacher what I need.

3. Speak in a kind and respectful way.

4. Follow directions.

Note About Procedures

Some of us feel resistant to formalizing procedural routines. It can feel like we're talking down to our students and making our classroom run more like a factory than a caring community. Factories turn out the same product repeatedly, but with our expectation for students to think and to be college and career ready, we need innovative thinkers who are responsible. That concern is a fair one. Know that the students can and should inform the creation and refinement of procedural routines. You don't want anything that happens in your classroom to be limited by your perspective. But students need to have some models, first. The best use of your and their time is for you to articulate as much as you can up front. But present it as a dialogue: when you introduce students to a new procedure, you explain that they're going to rehearse it as a way to make their time more efficient and that you're open to ideas of how to make it run even better. Students may provide suggestions for procedures or improvements to procedures that are not consistent with your vision, but using what students tell you gives them additional buy-in for following the procedure. It is often possible to tweak the suggestions so that your vision remains intact, but students have provided valued input. Developing procedural clarity will empower you and your students. The time you spend methodically teaching, modeling, practicing, and clarifying each expectation reduces the chance that valuable instruction time will be wasted with the need to regain momentum after disruption due to lack of clear understanding of the expectation.

Productive Instructional Time: Let's Learn!

Engaging learners can be achieved when, in tandem with productive noninstructional time, instructional time is also used productively. As you continue to read, strategies are suggested for making the most of your instructional time.

Whose Learning Is It?

When you make a conscious effort to help your students establish an authentic purpose for their learning, you establish relevance. *Relevance* and *authenticity* are jargon words thrown around in education. We can measure how effective we are at communicating relevance when students talk about their knowledge and relate their new learning to events that occur outside of the school setting. This discussion can be incorporated into the morning meeting news or into the school day at other times.

To improve students' engagement and learning, it is helpful to provide a purpose statement highlighting the relevance of the expected learning—the answer to "Why does this matter to me?" In their book *The Purposeful Classroom*, Frey and Fisher (2011) point out that the purpose for learning should be established in the initial introduction of the topic. This is helpful for the students because they know the target they are aiming for. It is also helpful for the teacher to frequently refer back to the purpose statement to be sure that instruction is focused as well. (See Figure 3–12 for ideas for developing your purpose statement.)

An alternative to providing a purpose statement is to involve students in developing the purpose. Students may be more motivated to reach the desired goal if they have input in deciding what that goal is. Here is an example given by Frey and Fisher (2011):

> Ms. Doyle's fifth-grade students agreed on a goal related to writing: To write three to five paragraphs for each of the teacher's prompts, with a total of three or fewer mistakes. Although this goal was part of a larger unit on quality writing that addressed voice, transitions, and thesis development, Ms. Doyle's students decided to focus on length and errors. Largely because they themselves set the focusing goal, they were able to improve on both of these aspects of their writing. (99)

Although helping students to develop and monitor learning goals can improve their motivation and increase their efficacy (Putnam and

Figure 3–12 Ideas for Developing Your Purpose Statement in Language That Supports ACCESS (Authentic, Collaborative, Challenging, End Product Understood, Self-Direction, Sustained Learning)

- Focus the purpose statement on learning rather than the learning activity.
- The purpose statement should include content and taxonomy demands of the standard that the objective is based on.
- Relevance is evident to students.
- Activities are aligned with the purpose statement.
- There is an understanding (teacher and student) of what mastery will look like (rubric or other assessment closely aligned with the objective).

Frey and Fisher (2011)

Walker 2010; Yamagishi and Houtekamer 2005), other types of goals are also very important. Particularly in the context of writing instruction, providing opportunities for students to establish goals that are relevant to an authentic purpose, allowing them to apply the skills they are learning to achieve some personally meaningful objective, is also critical (Duke 2010; Duke et al. 2006; Gambrell 2011; Purcell-Gates, Duke, and Martineau 2007; Sunger and Senler 2010). Writing instruction proceeds best when students are writing for the purpose for which that genre was intended and for an audience beyond the teacher. Writing to not make mistakes or learn to write better thesis statements is so much less compelling for students' development than, for example, writing a book to sell at a local store to raise money for a cause or writing a persuasive pamphlet for potential donors to a conservation organization, and so on (e.g., making real change in the world, not counting mechanical errors). Mechanical issues and thesis statements can be addressed, but in the context of that real-world purpose and audience for writing a real-world genre. Many examples are provided in the book, *Reading and Writing Genre with Purpose in K–8 Classrooms* (Duke et al. 2011).

Students Feel Responsible for Their Learning and Apply Learning Strategies

Once students understand the connections between learning, self, and life, students are in a position to accept responsibility for behavior and learning through self-regulation. Self-regulation—when students accept and maintain responsibility for their behavior and learning—provides huge benefits for both students and teachers, but we have to create opportunities for students to practice it. Parsons (2008) has suggested ACCESS (acronym for authentic, collaborative, challenging, end product understood, self-direction, sustained learning; see Figure 3–13 for suggested task traits for promoting self-regulation). Using authentic tasks in collaboration with other learners that provide a challenge (in the students' zone of proximal development) promotes self-regulation.

Figure 3–13 ACCESS: Task Traits That Promote Self-Regulation

A: Authentic tasks relevant to the learner
C: Collaboration with other students
C: Challenging tasks
E: End product understood by students
S: Self-direction
S: Sustained learning

Parsons (2008)

When students are given the opportunity to collaborate with their peers, they are able to "scaffold one another's literacy learning" (Parsons 2008, 630). When your instructional plan provides the opportunity for students to choose from several challenging activities, and this helps you provide instruction that is in your students' zone of proximal development. The instruction that you provide then results in a meaningful end product valued by your students. Whether the product is tangible or not, students are able to easily identify the purpose and the product for the learning they are constructing. Because they choose their activities, they self-direct their own learning, and students' learning is sustained. Sustained learning occurs for your students because your instructional activities require practice and interaction that is not accomplished in a single, isolated event. The learning is connected to authentic tasks; therefore, your students are able to transfer the learning beyond the classroom.

When you model using metacognitive self-questions (see Figure 3–14) and you move around the classroom monitoring students as they read, quietly checking in on students who have puzzled or distant looks or who are talking to their classmates before they have finished, you create a more independent, self-directed environment with you serving as a scaffold should students need assistance.

In addition, students benefit from practicing independent problem-solving procedures (see Figure 3–15). For example, as students work

Figure 3–14 Metacognitive Self-Questions

- What will it look like when I master the objective?
- How will I know that I have mastered the objective?
- What will I be able to do when I master the objective?
- Where will I go from there?

Figure 3–15 Problem-Solving Strategies

- If you don't know it, look it up in the text (may be dictionary, glossary, or other text).
- Ask three before me (the teacher). (Be sure you have clarified appropriate use of this one.)
- Reread the directions, text, question, and so on.
- Check to see if there are directions posted. For example, on the wall, there may be a sign that says, "When you are finished, you may. . . ."

independently, you continue to move around the room, listening to their discussions and modeling how to ask or answer questions as needed. Your modeling helps the students understand exactly what you are asking them to do and how to do it.

Note About Feedback

We hope you will find that, as research has suggested, providing specific feedback to your students helps them to identify their strengths, their areas for improvement, and their goals for their learning. Prensky (2010) suggests that you use the video game as a model for your feedback (and, in your case, this analogy serves as a kind of advance organizer for you as you read about assessment here!). In a video game, when a move is correct, the feedback is immediate. You provide feedback in a timely manner (today or tomorrow, as opposed to three weeks later). In a video game, feedback is focused on the specific event in the game. Your feedback is targeted and includes information related to students' successful performance and for improving. In a video game, the level that you are playing at is adjusted as needed so that you are playing at the correct level. For your students, you adjust your instruction based on the students' needs. You provide feedback in writing and in conversation and then target instruction to meet specific needs. By doing this, you enable your students to become increasingly self-regulated, and they take the feedback you give them as direction for their learning.

Moreover, frequent formal and informal assessments of your students' needs help you to determine appropriate levels of challenge for students so that individual needs are more likely to be met. You also carefully select the reading to be within most of your students' independent reading level, so that most students are not apt to get bored or struggle too much and then give up. You strategically group students so that there is a range of reading skill in each group, but no group represents the full range of the class; this allows students to assist one another before raising their hand to seek your assistance.

You also have to provide guidelines for students to provide feedback for each other. Because you have taken time to develop your classroom environment, students learn to trust each other. If you provide them with a protocol for providing feedback, then students are able to do this without offending each other. For example, you teach them to tell two likes and one improvement whenever they are providing feedback on their peers' work. Now, your feedback is not the only feedback that students value, so you have additional time to work with individuals as needed.

Students Know the Clear, Specific Goals and Can Self-Monitor
Students' self-regulation is supported when they know instructional time is organized around clear, specific goals, and they are able to monitor their own progress. Even very young elementary students can self-monitor, that is, identify their progress toward their learning goals (which is a key step in the bigger process of self-regulation). They understand

when they graph their own reading fluency that the line should go up because reading more correct words per minute is good. Once again, let's return to Ms. Hart—Ms. Hart micromanages her class, and her students perceive that she doesn't trust them. In self-evaluation, Ms. Hart realizes this is a problem in her class, so she tries a new strategy. Ms. Hart identifies her objectives, and then, based on the framework, she identifies several learning activities that are not only authentic but also aligned carefully with the objectives. Then, she considers how she will facilitate students' collaboration with each other. This requires her to trust her students to regulate their own learning and behavior, but she doesn't do this blindly. While planning her instruction, she also plans how she will teach students to collaborate (still using the CHAMPs framework for procedures).

Now, students see the rationale behind the learning activities as a result of Ms. Hart's attention to explaining and practicing procedural routines. This perception is also key to students' engagement and ownership of learning. She recognizes that she is able to make better use of her instructional time when her learning activities have been carefully designed with the end goal of students' mastery of learning objectives. In addition, Ms. Hart identifies specific learning needs of individuals and small groups of students. She plans carefully so that not only does she address the needs of the whole group, she also provides targeted instruction for those who are not mastering the objectives without the extra help. Students sense the importance of time on task when she does this.

In Section 1, Ms. Rodriguez analyzed the way time was used throughout the school day, and she realized that she might be able to make better use of up to 15 percent of available time. In addition to setting up daily procedures more efficiently, she thought about the ways that she might apply ACCESS to engage students and develop self-regulation at the same time. She recognized that authentic and relevant tasks would help students to see learning as relevant. The objective she was interested in teaching was stated as: "At the end of the unit of study, the student will be able to compare and contrast organisms in a wetland ecosystem and describe the ways they are interrelated by scoring 16 of 20 points on a given rubric." The unit included students researching the ecosystem to plan what they could expect to see, what they would want to see, and what samples they would like to collect during their upcoming wetlands field trip. The end product, following the field trip and additional research on the organisms they observed, would be presentations by groups of students in which they would be responsible for describing the relationships between the organisms using props and details from their field trip (photos, samples, etc.).

While Ms. Rodriguez designed the expectation for the end product, she used the ACCESS questions: Is this an authentic task related to real life? Yes. Will students have the opportunity to collaborate with other students? Yes. Is this a challenging assignment (but still doable)? Yes. Here she decided that her rubric would be very detailed and would be provided to the students at the beginning of the unit so that they could use it as a checklist for developing the product. Will students be able to understand the relevance of the end product? Yes. The end product would be presentations to first graders. Will students be required to self-direct (self-regulate) their learning? Yes, definitely. And will the completion of the process of developing the product lead to sustained learning? Yes. Now, Ms. Rodriguez felt confident that students would be engaged and believe that it mattered that they attended school that day.

Working Together

We have really enjoyed working together over the past couple years as educational researcher/professor (Alysia) and master teacher/graduate student (Beth), and as coauthors—especially writing this book! This is likely because we share a passion for improving the quality of teaching that students receive. We also have a mutual respect for one another that sometimes is not always as prevalent as it should be in K–12 or university settings. It is so important that the work of educational researchers and of educational practitioners inform and enhance one another. Teacher educators and researchers have been much criticized for apparent failures to link theory and research and practice (Korthagen 2007). School–university collaboration, which can start with collaborations between individuals (like ours that produced this book), may help us improve professional development, as well as our teaching and/or research. And continuous improvement of our practice may help to us provide the best opportunities for all children. We hope that this book and products of our other current and future collegial collaborations will help to

> ground scholarly research in practice and practice in scholarly research. Without such rootedness, researchers often misconstrue schools' pedagogical goals and fail to appreciate the nuances of practice, whereas educators often misunderstand scientific findings and are subject to the latest pseudoscientific claims of popular literature. (Kuriloff et al. 2009, 34)

AFTERWORD

ELLIN OLIVER KEENE

This morning I have taken seven pictures of my dogs lying in the sun in the front yard, ordered shoes online (that just can't be a good idea), and texted with my daughter. Why? Because I should be working on my next book and I have several other manuscripts to review. I have time wasting, or at least procrastination, honed to a fine art and I have seen similar "artists" at work in classrooms. They can shuffle paper, sharpen pencils, escape to the bathroom, and drive everyone else to distraction without anyone being the wiser. It's as if I had taught them myself, but I swear I didn't. . . .

I had aha moment after revelation after epiphany as I read this book. I was struck by the number of hours we lose each year and I became aware of the unintentional contributions we teachers make.

I am grateful that Beth and Alysia so clearly articulated how we can exercise preventative measures in classrooms and schools.

To me, though, the most important thread running through this book is the unwavering respect that these authors show for children. My takeaway is that students will rise to the occasion when the way is clearly shown. Beth and Alysia remind us that we can and should trust children to solve problems for themselves and emphasize that engaged, active learning is the ultimate goal. I can waste time with the best of them, but I didn't procrastinate in reading this book and I can't wait to share it with my colleagues around the country.

General Resources

Resource for	Resource	Information for Obtaining Resource
Time in schools	About academic learning time	Vockell, E. n.d. *Educational Psychology: A Practical Approach.* "Chapter 2, Using Time Effectively: The Secret to Successful Learning." Academic Learning Time. http://education.purduecal.edu/Vockell/EdPsyBook/Edpsy2/edpsy2_intro
	Expanded Learning Time Initiative	"ELT Initiative." Results & Research. www.mass2020.org/?q=node/72
	National Center on Time and Learning	"Research." www.timeandlearning.org/?q=research
Productive noninstructional time	*The Morning Meeting Book*	Kriete, R., and L. Bechtel. 2002. *The Morning Meeting Book.* Turners Falls, MA: Northeast Foundation for Children, Inc.
	Overview of the morning meeting	www.responsiveclassroom.org/sites/default/files/mm_overview.pdf
	Morning meeting greetings	"Greetings for Morning Meeting." http://wonder teacher.com/greetings-for-morning-meeting/
	The Essential 55	Clark, R. 2003. *The Essential 55.* New York: Hyperion.
	"A Framework for Building Schoolwide Community"	Casto, K. L., and J. R. Audley. 2008. "In Our School: Building Community in Elementary Schools." Introduction available at https://www.responsiveclassroom.org/sites/default/files/IOSintro.pdf

Appendix A: General Resources *(continued)*

Resource for	Resource	Information for Obtaining Resource
Productive noninstructional time *(continued)*	Conflict/Resolution Education website	"How to Use Class Meetings." Community Building. www.creducation.org /resources/class_meetings/community_building.html
	Team building in the classroom	"Organization Development: Team Building Blog." http://create-learning.com /blog/team-building/trust-happens-on-purpose-within-teams-workshop
	American Psychological Association: "Classroom Management"	"Modules Available: Search for classroom management." www.apa.org
	Responsive classroom start-up	Denton, P., and R. Kriete. 2000. "The First Six Weeks of School." Chapter 1 available at https://www.responsiveclassroom.org/sites/default /files/8904ch01.pdf
	CHAMPs references	"Safe and Civil Schools." www.safeandcivilschools.com/research/references /champs.php
Productive instructional time	*Making Standards Useful in the Classroom*	Marzano, R. J., and M. W. Haystead. 2008. *Making Standards Useful in the Classroom.* Alexandria, VA: ASCDR.
	Northwest Educational Technology Consortium research-based strategies	"Focus on Effectiveness: Integrating Technology into Research-based Strategies." www.netc.org/focus/
	"Math and English Essentials" video	"The Teaching Channel Presents: Math and English Essentials." www .teachingchannel.org/videos/tch-presents-make-learning-relevant
	Indiana K–6 Reading Framework	"Indiana K–6 Reading Framework: Instruction." www.doe.in.gov/sites/default /files/curriculum/2-reading-framework-instruction1.pdf

Assessment tools	Scholastic tools for self-assessment	Self-assessment Checklist." http://teacher.scholastic.com/professional/selfassessment/checklist/
	Classroom Time Analysis Tool	"Classroom Time Analysis Tool (CTAT) Login." http://ctat.nctl.iontier.com/Login.aspx?ReturnUrl=%2f
	Student Engagement: Teacher Handbook	Jones, R. D. 2009. "Student Engagement Student Handbook." Available at www.leadered.com/pdf/Student%20Engage%20handbook%20excerpt.pdf
		(This article includes tools for assessing student engagement.)
	"Measuring Student Engagement in Upper Elementary Through High School: A Description of 21 Instruments"	http://ies.ed.gov/ncee/edlabs/regions/southeast/pdf/REL_2011098.pdf
		(This publication summarizes twenty-one tools for measuring student engagement.)

APPENDIX B

Transition Ideas

Title	Idea	Source
Cracker Facts	Keep vocabulary and previous learning fact questions on notecards (shaped like crackers) in a cracker box. During transitions that need time (bathroom, snack, prep to go home/lunch/special area), ask the questions on the cards as a game for students (earn points or other rewards for table team or individual).	Lindemann, A. "Transition Ideas in the Elementary Classroom." eHow. www.ehow.com/info_7967520 _transition-ideas-elementary-classroom.html
Morning news and predictable expectations	Provide predictable routines for entry into the classroom with procedures posted including practice work for the morning.	"Transition Activities and Tips." The Cornerstone RSS. http://thecornerstoneforteachers.com/free -resources/routines-and-procedures/transition-tips
Regular routines	Use timers, tells, bell/chime, clicker, signal indicators for transitions.	
Student teacher box or journals	Students provide feedback and ideas for the teacher.	
I Love That Teaching Idea	This site provides many ideas for teachers related to classroom management and transitions.	"Give Them Ownership." www.ilovethatteachingidea .com/ideas/050105_give_them_ownership.htm
Easy transition activities	This site provides quick ideas for transitioning in the classroom.	"Five Easy Transition Activities." www.glencoe .com/sec/teachingtoday/downloads/pdf /transitionactivities1.pdf

Appendix B: Transition Ideas (continued)

Title	Idea	Source
Music for transition	Use a fifteen-second song with procedure attached to expected behavior.	YouTube. "Come to the Carpet." www.youtube.com/watch?v=Wd5xLpGRvVo
Vocabulary word of the day	Tell meaning of the word and give page number; students raise hand when they have located the word on the page.	(Many ideas in video) YouTube. "Transition Tips for Teachers." www.youtube.com/watch?v=umQeTEUKjiU
Two claps and a snap	When students transition from one activity to another, they sometimes get distracted by the activity of others. The teacher may quietly say, "two claps and a snap." Then, students who are paying attention to what the teacher is saying join in with the teacher to clap twice and snap their fingers once. Others return attention to the teacher.	Other ideas at "I Love That Teaching Idea." www.ilovethatteachingidea.com/ideas/032404_get_the_noise_out.htm
Cooper Says	This idea is taken from an activity in *The Morning Meeting Book* (p. 184). The teacher quietly begins giving a series of quick "Cooper says hands on shoulders; Cooper says touch your front; Cooper says touch your chin; touch your ears. . . . Cooper didn't say," and so on. Students begin to join in quickly. This is similar to Simon Says, but nobody is out while students' attention is regained.	Kriete, R., and L. Bechtel. 2002. *The Morning Meeting Book.* Turners Falls, MA: Northeast Foundation for Children, Inc.

A note about transitions: As with any procedure you attempt, the success of transitions will depend on the clarity of the expectation. When teaching transitions, remember to identify how the students will know it is time to transition (signal, music, whatever), be specific about procedure for transitioning, model, check for understanding, and practice with feedback. Then, implement the transition procedure and provide additional feedback and practice as needed.

REFERENCES

Amrein, A. L., and D. C. Berliner. 2002. "High-Stakes Testing, Uncertainty, and Student Learning." *Education Policy Analysis Archives* 10. Available at http://epaa.asu.edu/epaa/v10n18/.

Armendariz, F., and J. Umbreit. 1999. "Using Active Responding to Reduce Disruptive Behavior in a General Education Classroom." *Journal of Positive Behavior Interventions* 1: 152–58.

Bennett, R. E. 2011. "Formative Assessment: A Critical Review." *Assessment in Education: Principles, Policy & Practice* 18: 5–25.

Berliner, D. C. 1990. "What's All the Fuss About Instructional Time?" In *The Nature of Time in Schools: Theoretical Concepts, Practitioner Perceptions*, ed. M. Ben-Peretz and R. Bromme. New York: Teachers College Press.

Bohn, C. M., A. D. Roehrig, and M. Pressley. 2004. "The First Days of School in the Classrooms of Two More Effective and Four Less Effective Primary-Grades Teachers." *The Elementary School Journal* 104 (4): 269–87.

Brooks, D. M. 1985. "The Teacher's Communicative Competence: The First Day of School." *Theory into Practice* 24: 63–70.

Carlisle, J. F., and D. Berebitsky. 2011. "Literacy Coaching as a Component of Professional Development." *Reading and Writing: An Interdisciplinary Journal* 24: 773–800.

Cassetta, G., and B. Sawyer. 2013. *No More Taking Away Recess and Other Problematic Discipline Practices*. Portsmouth, NH: Heinemann.

Casto, K. L., and J. R. Audley. 2008. *In Our School*. Turner Falls, MA: Northeast Foundation for Children, Inc.

Chalk, K., and L. A. Bizo. 2004. "Specific Praise Improves On-Task Behaviour and Numeracy Enjoyment: A Study of Year 4 Pupils Engaged in the Numeracy Hour." *Educational Psychology in Practice* 20: 335–52.

Cheyne, J. A., and D. Tarulli. 1999. "Dialogue, Difference, and the 'Third Voice' in the Zone of Proximal Development." *Theory and Psychology* 9: 5–28.

Clark, R. 2003. *The Essential 55*. New York: Hyperion.

Clunies-Ross, P., E. Little, and M. Kienhuis. 2008. "Self-Reported and Actual Use of Proactive and Reactive Classroom Management Strategies and Their Relationship with Teacher Stress and Student Behavior." *Educational Psychology: An International Journal of Experimental Educational Psychology* 28: 693–710.

Colvin, G., G. Sugai, R. H. Good III, and Y.-Y. Lee. 1997. "Using Active Supervision and Precorrection to Improve Transition Behaviors in an Elementary School." *School Psychology Quarterly* 12: 344–61.

Connor, C. M., F. J. Morrison, B. J. Fishman, C. Schatschneider, and P. Underwood. 2007. "The Early Years: Algorithm-Guided Individualized Reading Instruction." *Science* 315: 464–65.

Connor, C. M., S. B. Piasta, B. Fishman, S. Glasney, C. Schatschneider, E. Crowe, P. Underwood, and F. J. Morrison. 2009. "Individualizing Student Instruction Precisely: Effects of Child by Instruction Interactions on First Graders' Literacy Development." *Child Development* 80 (1): 77–100.

Cordova, D. I., and M. R. Lepper. 1996. "Intrinsic Motivation and the Process of Learning: Beneficial Effects of Contextualization, Personalization, and Choice." *Journal of Educational Psychology* 88: 715–30.

Council on School Health. 2013. "The Crucial Role of Recess in School." *Pediatrics* 131: 183–88.

Dee, T. S., B. Jacob, and N. L. Schwartz. 2013. "The Effects of NCLB on School Resources and Practices." *Educational Evaluation and Policy Analysis* 35 (2): 252–79.

Duke, N. K. 2010. "The Real-World Reading and Writing U.S. Children Need." *The Phi Delta Kappan* 91 (5): 68–71.

Duke, N. K., S. Caughlan, M. M. Juzwik, and N. M. Martin. 2011. *Reading and Writing Genre with Purpose in K–8 Classrooms*. Portsmouth, NH: Heinemann.

Duke, N. K., V. Purcell-Gates, L. A. Hall, and C. Tower. 2006. "Authentic Literacy Activities for Developing Comprehension and Writing." *The Reading Teacher* 60 (4): 344–55.

Emmer, E. T., C. M. Evertson, and L. M. Anderson. 1980. "Effective Classroom Management at the Beginning of the School Year." *The Elementary School Journal* 80 (5): 219–31.

Evertson, C. M. 1989. "Improving Elementary Classroom Management: A School-Based Training Program for Beginning the Year." *The Journal of Educational Research* 83 (2): 82–90.

Evertson, C. M., and E. T. Emmer. 1982. "Effective Management at the Beginning of the School Year in Junior High Classes." *Journal of Educational Psychology* 74: 485–98.

Fisher, D. 2009. "The Use of Instructional Time in the Typical High School Classroom." *The Educational Forum* 73 (2): 168–76.

Florez, I. R. 2011. "Developing Young Children's Self-Regulation Through Everyday Experiences." *Young Children* 66 (4): 46–51.

Freiberg, H. J., T. A. Stein, and S.-Y. Huang. 1995. "Effects of a Classroom Management Intervention on Student Achievement in Inner-City Elementary Schools." *Educational Research and Evaluation: An International Journal on Theory and Practice* 1: 36–66.

Frey, N., and N. Fisher. 2011. *The Purposeful Classroom: How to Structure Lessons with Learning Goals in Mind.* Alexandria, VA: ASCD.

Fuchs, L. S., D. Fuchs, C. L. Hamlett, and P. M. Stecker. 1991. "Effects of Curriculum-Based Measurement and Consultation on Teaching Planning and Student Achievement in Mathematics Operations." *American Educational Research Journal* 28: 617–41.

Fudge, D. L., C. H. Skinner, J. L. Williams, D. Cowden, J. Clark, and S. L. Bliss. 2008. "Increasing On-Task Behavior in Every Student in a Second-Grade Classroom During Transitions: Validating the Color Wheel System." *Journal of School Psychology* 46: 575–92.

Gambrell, L. B. 2011. "Seven Rules of Engagement: What's Most Important to Know About Motivation to Read." *The Reading Teacher* 65 (3): 172–78.

Gettinger, M., and M. J. Walter. 2012. "Classroom Strategies to Enhance Academic Engaged Time." In *Handbook of Research on Student Engagement*, ed. S. L. Christenson, A. L. Reschly, and C. Wylie, 653–73. New York: Springer.

Guthrie, J. T. 2001. "Contexts for Engagement and Motivation in Reading." *Reading Online* 4 (8). Available at www.readingonline.org /articles/art_index.asp?HREF=/articles/handbook/guthrie/index.html.

Guthrie, J. T., A. Wigfield, P. Barbosa, K. C. Perencevich, A. Taboada, M. H. Davis, N. T. Scafiddi, and S. Tonks. 2004. "Increasing Reading Comprehension and Engagement Through Concept-Oriented Reading Instruction." *Journal of Educational Psychology* 96: 403–23.

Hamre, B. K., and R. C. Pianta. 2005. "Can Instructional and Emotional Support in the First-Grade Classroom Make a Difference for Children at Risk of School Failure?" *Child Development* 76: 949–67.

Hamre, B. K., R. C. Pianta, J. T. Downer, J. DeCoster, A. J. Mashburn, and A. Hamagami. 2013. "Teaching Through Interactions: Testing a Developmental Framework of Teacher Effectiveness in over 4,000 Classrooms." *The Elementary School Journal* 113: 461–87.

Hattie, J. 2003. *Teachers Make a Difference: What Is the Research Evidence? Distinguishing Experts from Novice Teachers.* Available at www .decd.sa.gov.au/limestonecoast/files/pages/new%20page/PLC/teachers _make_a_difference.pdf.

Hofferth, S. L., and J. F. Sandberg. 2001. "How American Children Spend Their Time." *Journal of Marriage and Family* 63: 295–308.

Horn, M. B., and M. Evans. 2013. "A Factory Model for Schools No Longer Works." *Journal Sentinel Online*, 29 June. Available at www .jsonline.com/news/opinion/a-factory-model-for-schools-no-longer -works-b9943187z1-213602131.html.

Hughes, J. N., W. Wu, and S. G. West. 2011. "Teacher Performance Goal Practices and Elementary Students' Behavioral Engagement: A Developmental Perspective." *Journal of School Psychology* 49 (1): 1–23.

Kolbe, T., M. Partridge, and F. O'Reilly. 2011. *Time and Learning in Schools: A National Profile.* Available at www.timeandlearning.org/files /SASS.pdf.

Korthagen, F. A. 2007. "The Gap Between Research and Practice Revisited." *Educational Research and Evaluation* 13: 303–10.

Kriete, R., and L. Bechtel. 2002. *The Morning Meeting Book.* Turners Falls, MA: Northeast Foundation for Children.

Kuriloff, P., M. Reichert, B. Stoudt, and S. Ravitch. 2009. "Building Research Collaboratives Among Schools and Universities: Lessons from the Field." *Mind, Brain, and Education* 2: 34–44.

Langer, J. A. 2001. "Succeeding Against the Odds in English." *The English Journal* 91: 37–42.

Locke, E. A., and G. P. Latham. 2002. "Building a Practically Useful Theory of Goal Setting and Task Motivation: A 35-Year Odyssey." *American Psychologist* 57 (9): 705–17.

Lüftenegger, M., B. Schober, R. van de Schoot, P. Wagner, M. Finsterwald, and C. Spiel. 2012. "Lifelong Learning as a Goal—Do Autonomy and Self-Regulation in School Result in Well Prepared Pupils?" *Learning and Instruction* 22 (1): 27–36.

Marzano, R. J., and M. W. Haystead. 2008. *Making Standards Useful in the Classroom.* Alexandria, VA: Association for Supervision and Curriculum Development.

McDonald, A. S. 2001. "The Prevalence and Effects of Test Anxiety in School Children." *Educational Psychology: An International Journal of Experimental Educational Psychology* 21 (1): 89–101.

McLaughlin, M., D. J. McGrath, M. A. Burian-Fitzgerald, L. Lanahan, M. Scotchmer, C. Enyeart, and L. Salganik. 2005. *Student Content Engagement as a Construct for the Measurement of Effective*

Classroom Instruction and Teacher Knowledge. Washington, DC: American Institutes for Research. Available at www.air.org/files /AERA2005Student_Content_Engagement11.pdf.

McTigue, E. M., and S. E. Rimm-Kaufman. 2010. "The Responsive Classroom Approach and Its Implications for Improving Reading and Writing." *Reading and Writing Quarterly: Overcoming Learning Difficulties* 27: 5–24.

Michalsky, T., Z. R. Mevarech, and L. Haibi. 2013. "Elementary School Children Reading Scientific Texts: Effects of Metacognitive Instruction." *The Journal of Educational Research* 102: 363–76.

Morton, B., and B. Dalton. 2007. *Changes in Instructional Hours in Four Subjects by Public School Teachers of Grades 1 Through 4.* Washington, DC: U.S. Department of Education, National Center for Education Statistics. Available at http://nces.ed.gov/pubs2007/2007305.pdf.

Nichols, S. L., and H. S. Dawson. 2012. "Assessment as a Context for Student Engagement." In *Handbook of Research on Student Engagement,* ed. S. L. Christenson, A. M. Reschly, and C. Wylie, 457–77. New York: Springer.

Palincsar, A. S. 2007. "The Role of Research, Theory, and Representation in the Transformation of Instructional Research." *National Reading Conference Yearbook* 67: 41–52.

Palincsar, A. S., and A. L. Brown. 1984. "Reciprocal Teaching of Comprehension-Fostering and Comprehension-Monitoring Activities." *Cognition and Instruction* 1 (2): 117–75.

Parsons, S. A. 2008. "Providing All Students ACCESS to Self-Regulated Literacy Learning." *The Reading Teacher* 61: 628–35.

Pianta, R. C., J. B. Belsky, N. Vandergrift, R. Houts, and F. J. Morrison. 2008. "Classroom Effects on Children's Achievement Trajectories in Elementary School." *American Educational Research Journal* 45: 365–97.

Pintrich, P. R., and E. V. De Groot. 1990. "Motivational and Self-Regulated Learning Components of Classroom Academic Performance." *Journal of Educational Psychology* 82: 33–40.

Prensky, M. 2010. *Teaching Digital Natives: Partnering for Real Learning.* Thousand Oaks, CA: Corwin.

Pressley, M., S. E. Dolezal, L. M. Raphael, L. Mohan, A. D. Roehrig, and K. Bogner. 2003. *Motivating Primary-Grade Students.* New York: Guilford.

Pressley, M., A. D. Roehrig, L. M. Raphael, S. E. Dolezal, C. Bohn, L. Mohan, R. Wharton-McDonald, K. Bogner, and K. Hogan. 2003. "Teaching Processes in Elementary and Secondary Education." In *Handbook of Psychology,* Volume 7: *Educational Psychology,* ed. W. M. Reynolds, and G. E. Miller, 153–75. New York: John Wiley and Sons.

Pulfrey C., C. Darnon, and F. Butera. 2013. "Autonomy and Task Performance: Explaining the Impact of Grades on Intrinsic Motivation." *Journal of Educational Psychology* 105 (1): 39–57.

Purcell-Gates, N. K. Duke, and J. A. Martineau. 2007. "Learning to Read and Write Genre-Specific Text: Roles of Authentic Experience and Explicit Teaching." *Reading Research Quarterly* 42 (1): 8–45.

Putnam, M., and C. Walker. 2011. "Motivating Children to Read and Write: Using Informal Learning Environments as Contexts for Literacy Instruction." *Journal of Research in Childhood Education* 24: 140–51.

Roehrig, A. D., E. H. Brinkerhoff, E. S. Rawls, and T. Pressley. 2013. "Motivating Classroom Practices to Support Effective Literacy Instruction." In *Effective Literacy Instruction: A Handbook of Practice,* ed. N. Duke and B. M. Taylor, 13–45. New York: Guilford.

Roehrig, A. D., and E. Christesen. 2010. "Development and Use of a Tool for Evaluating Teacher Effectiveness in Grades K–12." In *Innovative Assessment for the 21st Century,* ed. V. J. Shute and B. J. Becker, 207–28. New York: Springer.

Roehrig, A. D., J. E. Turner, M. Arrastia, E. Christesen, S. McElhaney, and L. Jakiel. 2012. "Effective Teachers and Teaching: Characteristics and Practices Related to Student Outcomes." In *Educational Psychology Handbook,* Volume 2: *Individual Differences, Cultural Variations, and Contextual Factors in Educational Psychology,* ed.

T. Urdan, S. Graham, M. Royer, and M. Zeidner, 501–27. Washington, DC: American Psychological Association.

Rosenshine, B., and C. Meister. 1994. "Reciprocal Teaching: A Review of the Research." *Review of Educational Research* 64 (4): 479–530.

Ryan, R. M., and E. L. Deci. 2000. "Intrinsic and Extrinsic Motivations: Classic Definitions and New Directions." *Contemporary Educational Psychology* 25: 54–67. doi:10.1006/ceps.1999.1020.

Schunk, D. H. 2008. *Learning Theories: An Educational Perspective*, 5th ed. New York: Pearson.

Shepard, L. A., and K. C. Dougherty. 1991. "Effects of High-Stakes Testing on Instruction." Paper presented at the annual meeting of the American Educational Research Association and the National Council on Measurement in Education, April 3–7, Chicago, IL. Available at www.colorado.edu/UCB/AcademicAffairs/education/faculty/lorrie shepard/PDF/Effects%20of%20High-Stakes%20Testing.pdf.

Shute, V. J. 2008. "Focus on Formative Feedback." *Review of Educational Research* 78: 153–89.

Simonsen, B., S. Fairbanks, A. Briesch, D. Myers, and G. Sugai. 2008. "Evidence-Based Practices in Classroom Management: Considerations for Research to Practice." *Education and Treatment of Children* 31: 351–80.

Smith, B. A. 2000. "Quantity Matters: Annual Instruction Time in an Urban School System." *Educational Administration Quarterly* 36: 652–82.

Smith, M. L., and C. Rottenberg. 2005. "Unintended Consequences of External Testing in Elementary Schools." *Educational Measurement Issues and Practice* 10 (4): 7–11.

Sprick, R., M. Garrison, and L. M. Howard. 1998. *CHAMPs: A Proactive and Positive Approach to Classroom Management for Grades K–9*. Longmount, CO: Sopris West.

Sunger, S., and B. Senler. 2010. "Students' Achievement Goals in Relation to Academic Motivation, Competence Expectancy, and

Classroom Environment Perceptions." *Educational Research and Evaluation: An International Journal on Theory and Practice* 16 (4): 303–24.

Taylor, B. M. 2011. *Catching Schools: An Action Guide to Schoolwide Reading Improvement.* Portsmouth, NH: Heinemann.

Taylor, B. M., P. D. Pearson, K. Clark, and S. Walpole. 2000. "Effective Schools and Accomplished Teachers: Lessons About Primary Grade Reading Instruction in Low-Income Schools." *Elementary School Journal* 101: 121–65.

Tharp, R. G., P. Estrada, S. S. Dalton, and L. A. Yamauchi. 2000. *Teaching Transformed: Achieving Excellence, Fairness, Inclusion, and Harmony.* Boulder, CO: Westview.

Tschannen-Moran, M., A. W. Hoy, and W. K. Hoy. 1998. "Teacher Efficacy: Its Meaning and Measure." *Review of Educational Research* 68: 202–48.

Vansteenkiste, M., J. Simons, W. Lens, K. M. Sheldon, and E. L. Deci. 2004. "Motivating Learning, Performance, and Persistence: The Synergistic Role of Intrinsic Goals and Autonomy-Support." *Journal of Personality and Social Psychology* 87: 246–60.

Vygotsky, L. S. 1978. *Mind and Society: The Development of Higher Psychological Processes.* Cambridge, MA: Harvard University Press.

Wasson, B. B., P. L. Beare, and J. B. Wasson. 1990. "Classroom Behavior of Good and Poor Readers." *Journal of Educational Research* 83 (3): 162–65.

Watson, M., and V. Battistich. 2006. "Building and Sustaining Caring Communities." In *Handbook of Classroom Management: Research, Practice, and Contemporary Issues,* ed. C. M. Evertson and C. S. Weinstein, 253–79. New York: Routledge.

Wharton-McDonald, R., M. Pressley, and J. M. Hampston. 1998. "Outstanding Literacy Instruction in First Grade: Teacher Practices and Student Achievement." *Elementary School Journal* 99: 101–128.

Wigfield, A., J. T. Guthrie, K. C. Perencevich, A. Taboada, S. L. Klauda, A. McRae, and P. Barbosa. 2008. "The Role of Reading Engagement in Mediating Effects of Reading Comprehension Instruction on Reading Outcomes." *Psychology in the Schools* 45: 432–45.

Wigfield, A., J. T. Guthrie, S. Tonks, and K. C. Perencevich. 2004. "Children's Motivation for Reading: Domain Specificity and Instructional Influences." *Journal of Educational Research* 97: 299–309.

Yamagishi, R., and T. Houtekamer. 2005. "Assessment and Goal-Setting with the Circle of Courage." *Reclaiming Children and Youth* 14 (3): 160–63.